Ask Barney

Got a Question about the Casino?
Any Question at All?

Ask Barney

An Insider's Guide to Las Vegas

Barney Vinson
Edited by David P. Tarino

Bonus Books, Inc.
Chicago, Illinois

06   05   04   03   02   5   4   3   2   1

Library of Congress Control Number 2002100374

ISBN 1-56625-181-8

Bonus Books, Inc.
160 E. Illinois St.
Chicago, IL 60611

Printed in the United States of America

As always, to Debbie.

Table of Contents

Welcome to
Las Vegas

Welcome to Las Vegas—the city of lights, the land of dreams, the entertainment capital of the world, the place where time stands still. It's the last true frontier town in the Old West, only you're not drawing against the fastest gun in the territory. You're up against an even more formidable opponent: the casino. That can be absolutely terrifying! I know, because I felt the same way when I came to Las Vegas in 1967. Back then, it was a small town, and yet I was still shaking in my boots.

But over the years I've learned one thing. Las Vegas is more a state of mind than an actual place. From shill to dealer to floor supervisor to gaming instructor at Caesars Palace, I've heard all the questions.

"Do you live in the hotel?"

"What time is the midnight show?"

"Do these stairs go up?"

And my very favorite:

"Is it okay to gamble if you don't know what you're doing?"

My answer was, "Sure! The casinos love that."

The problem is that most of us are intimidated by casinos. That's why slot machines are so popular. You can play at your own pace without anybody staring at you, and occasionally even get money back.

My mother-in-law loves slot machines. Every time she

walks into a casino, she looks at the banks of slot machines with a big smile on her face and says, "Oh boy, a smorgasbord!"

In fact, on one of her recent trips to Las Vegas she played the slot machines for nine hours straight. When she called my wife, she automatically put five quarters in the telephone!

For most of us, though, there is something sinister about being inside a casino. It isn't the cheap food and roller coaster rides and video arcades. It's gambling itself, which goes against everything we've ever been taught. You're supposed to work for your money, not get it by betting on a basketball game or a roll of the dice. Fortunately for the casinos, however, there's a streak of larceny inside each of us, and the idea of getting money without actually working for it appeals to just about everybody.

There's also the fact that when your money's on the line, everything else becomes secondary—at least for the moment. You've got dental surgery next week; your cat ran away from home; someone else got the promotion that should have been yours. But here you are at the blackjack table, $20 riding on one hand. You're staring at a 9 and a 6, and the dealer's showing a 10. You scratch for another card, and the only thing you're thinking about is what that next card will be.

Think of gambling as entertainment, in its rawest and purest form. Don't worry about pit bosses and the eye in the sky, and all the other shadowy casino terminology I will explain in this book. In fact, I'm going to answer every casino question you could possibly think of— starting with the number one question that everybody always asks:

Why are casino dealers so rude and surly?

I've noticed that a rude and surly dealer is usually preceded by a rude and surly player. But it's like any other job. There are good doctors and bad doctors. There are good plumbers and bad plumbers. There are bad lawyers, and worse lawyers.

Most dealers are cheerful and polite, and they darn well better be. Casinos today stress courtesy and customer satisfaction above anything else. Complain to the pit boss about a dealer, and that dealer is in big trouble.

There are several things you can do to ensure that the dealer won't be rude to you. First, treat the dealer like you want to be treated. When you sit down at the table, smile and say hello. Other conversation starters include "How are you?" and "Has it been busy today?"

Avoid such time-worn phrases as "You look bored" or "How come you never smile?" (One dealer's answer to this was "Because you ain't funny!")

Don't blame the dealer when you lose. He has no control over the cards, dice, or roulette ball—and he's not rooting for the casino any more than you are. In fact, if you're not sure what to do when you're playing, ask the dealer for help. (Most of them are just like humans.)

When all else fails, tip the dealer. They only make minimum wage, and a tip is money in their pocket. You can either tip the dealer, or make a bet for him. He prefers a bet, because he gets twice as much money if he wins.

If you're on a limited budget, here's an economical way to tip. Wait until one dealer is sending another on a break. Then tip. One dealer gets the money, another dealer sees that you tipped, and you've killed two birds with one stone!

Do dealers get to keep their tips?

Poker dealers usually do, but just about every other dealer has to put his tips in a community "toke box," or tip box. The tips are usually divided every 24 hours by the number of dealers who worked that day. Because of I.R.S.

tax compliance laws, most casinos will issue tips in the form of a check, with all the taxes already taken out.

So if you give a dealer a tip, he will get only a fraction of that money, but it's still a nice gesture on your part.

Why aren't dealers allowed to keep their own tips?

According to management, it's more equitable to share the tips equally among all the dealers. After all, some tables are in better locations than others and will attract more players. (More players, more tips.) There's also the fact that the dealer on a $25 game will get bigger tips than the dealer on a $1 game. The big problem, however, is that if a dealer is allowed to keep all his tips, he's more inclined to hustle bets for himself, which is a flagrant violation of casino policy.

Here's what happened at one Strip hotel a few years ago. One of the players won a lot of money and was preparing to leave the table. A young inexperienced dealer whispered to him, "Don't forget the dealers."

"I won't," the player answered happily. "I'm going to play at your table from now on!"

Personally, I think each dealer should be allowed to keep his own tips. After all, if a dealer has a personal financial stake in the game, he'll do anything he can to keep the game going. If his money is being shared with several hundred other people, what does he care whether the game has any players or not?

By studying statistics, you'll find that dice games began to lose popularity in the mid-1980s—which is around the time when most crap dealers were forced to pool their tips. In fact, this was probably one of the main reasons why the mighty Dunes Hotel closed in 1993.

Until the early 1980s, the Dunes was one of the city's premiere gaming resorts. All the big action was at the dice tables, which were jammed with high rollers seven days a week. The hotel was making a fortune, and so were the dealers.

The players didn't mind, though. Most of them were hustlers themselves, and it was fun being hustled by someone else for a change. It was also a heady feeling to be recognized by the dealers as soon as you walked through the door, and knowing your favorite dice crew would get you a nice spot at the table no matter how crowded it was.

Sometimes you won, and you didn't mind if the dealers made a killing. Sometimes you lost, but there was always tomorrow, and one more chance to win it all back.

It was pure magic, and a magic that touched every other part of the casino. But then some corporate bean counter made an amazing discovery. The casino was making money, yes, but look at all the money the dealers were taking home—money the casino would never see again.

So in 1983 the dice dealers were forced to pool their tips. The result was that the dealers' income plummeted by 80%. The good dealers quit and got other jobs. Without good dealers, the good players quit coming. By the end of the decade, the dice pit was a graveyard, and so was the Dunes.

We met a nice dealer in Las Vegas and invited him to stay at our home on his vacation. How should we prepare his room?

Make sure his army cot is nice and firm. Leave lots of comic books on his night stand so he'll have plenty to read. Have a telephone in his room so he can check in daily with his probation officer. And by all means, hide the whiskey.

What is a pit boss?

Most people think that anyone wearing a suit is a pit boss. There's only one pit boss in each blackjack or dice pit, and he's the boss in that pit. All the others are floor supervisors. Now that corporations are running Las Vegas, however, there's no such thing as a pit boss. He's either called a games director or pit manager. It sounds a little more refined. And he isn't in the gambling business, either. He's in the gaming industry.

It's easy to differentiate between a pit boss and a floor supervisor. The floor supervisor is the one in the yellow jacket with the purple slacks and white socks. The pit boss is the one in the bright blue jacket with the orange slacks and no socks.

Why do pit bosses sweat the money at the tables?

Just because the pit boss is watching the game doesn't mean he's "sweating" the money. It's his job to watch the games. Another of his responsibilities is to make sure there are plenty of chips on the tables and to order "fills" when needed. The pit boss also has to account to his bosses when a table loses a large amount of money. Truthfully, he doesn't care whether the table loses or not. Chances are that if one table is blowing a lot of money, there are 15 others that are beating everybody's socks off.

Where is the best place to eat in a casino?

Ask yourself this question. Do you want someone with a French accent hovering over you while you try to read a velvet-encased menu by candlelight, or do you want to plunk down a $10 bill and eat everything in sight? I thought so.

Every casino worth its salt (and pepper) has a buffet. You get to eat as much as you want, and—unlike some gourmet restaurants—you get the food during the same calendar year. If you don't like what you get, shove your plate to one side and go get something else.

There's an art to eating in a buffet, so let's go over the proper way to attack one of these gastronomical emporiums. Don't load your plate with starchy foods like bread, pasta, and potatoes. Likewise hamburgers, french fries, pizza, sandwich meats, fish sticks, coleslaw, and fried chicken. You can get this stuff at a fast food joint. Why fill up on it at a nice buffet?

The first order of business is selecting the proper plate. The salad plates are stacked right next to the dinner plates, and are much smaller. Get a dinner plate, and then skip the salads altogether. Instead, be on the lookout for jumbo shrimp and crab legs, imported fruit, caviar, and other costly foods. In fact, you might do well to case the whole buffet beforehand. There's nothing more exasperating than loading your plate with lasagna and then finding New York steaks at the next counter.

According to my Uncle Frank, the biggest mistake most buffet patrons make is filling their plates improperly. He says the small items should go on the bottom, and the larger items on top. This will keep everything intact while your wife helps you carry your plate back to the table. And what big items should go on top? Why, the prime rib and ham sliced off the bone at the carving station! This is the primo stuff, and everything else should be secondary.

Save room for dessert. Vegas buffets are famous for their pies, cakes, and other pastries. Some even have flaming dessert stations where you can pig out on peach Melba, cherries jubilee, and plums with brandy sauce.

The best time to hit the buffet is when it first opens. Lines aren't as long, and you won't find lettuce floating in the salad dressing.

How do I know if a buffet is worth the money?

Tell the hostess you want to check out the food before you pay. People do it all the time.

> If the meat carver gives you a piece of prime rib you can practically see through, slip him a dollar. He'll slice you enough meat to feed everyone in your family.

How many buffets are there in Las Vegas?

As this goes to press, around 50 casinos have buffets that range in price from $4 to over $20. Pick up a Vegas newspaper for times and prices. There are also more than 30 weekend brunches around town, some offering unlimited champagne and other alcoholic drinks. The best of these is Bally's Sunday Sterling Brunch. It's also the most expensive, at over 50 bucks a person. Make reservations for this one.

How many food selections are featured at a Las Vegas buffet?

The average buffet features about 45 food selections, but don't put them all on one plate. Use two plates.

What was the first casino in Las Vegas to offer a buffet?

Let's look in the old history book. Ah, here it is on page 347 under "Heartburn." Beldon Katleman, who bought the El Rancho Vegas from builder Tommy Hull, was trying to find a way to keep customers in his hotel after the second show. The idea he came up with was "The Midnight Chuck Wagon Buffet—All You Can Eat For A Dollar!" Of course, imitation is the sincerest form of flattery, especially in Las Vegas, so the next night every other casino in town had a buffet.

What other great food bargains can I find in Las Vegas?

The best food bargain in town is the early morning breakfast, available in some of the smaller casinos between midnight and 6 a.m. In order to get you inside the casino, these places put out a lavish breakfast for as little as 50¢. Check newspaper ads or hotel marquees.

Another great bargain is the famous Vegas shrimp cocktail. One of the best around is at the Golden Gate, which goes through two tons of shrimp a week! Served in an old-fashioned sundae glass, it's 99¢, and probably the best food value in town.

Here's another money-saving idea. Order iced tea with your dinner, and take advantage of free refills. You'll save big bucks by not drinking wine or mixed drinks, which is where restaurants make much of their profit.

What if I get a bad meal in a restaurant?

If it happens (and it will), tell the waitress right away and then order something else. Under no condition should you ever send food back to the kitchen. Some cooks have no sense of humor. Here's how Max Rubin summed it up in his book *Comp City*: "You'll get the same plate reheated with at least one foreign object from the cook's body tucked in the food somewhere." Argh, check please!

What is a junket?

A junket is a casino package, usually arranged by either an independent junket representative (who's paid a commission for each person he brings to the casino) or by the casino itself. But don't confuse today's Vegas junkets with those of the 1970s, when each junket player got full comp privileges including free airfare. Today's junkets will cost you, but the advantage is that your airfare and room are usually included.

The disadvantage is that other amenities, such as meals and shows, are not part of the deal—unless your average bet and time spent gambling warrant these casino perks.

Consequently, many junketeers find themselves pressured to gamble more than they ordinarily would, which can turn a vacation into a nightmare. Most experts agree that you're better off to skip junket packages and travel on your own. Other advice:

- Pay for your airline ticket well in advance. (You'll save money.)
- Plan to check out of your hotel by the weekend. (Rooms are at a premium then and so are the prices.)
- Study up on your favorite game before you get to the casino. You wouldn't buy a stock without knowing something about the company. Don't gamble without doing your homework.

What is the best free show in Las Vegas?

Watching the expression on someone's face when he wins $20 million on a Megabucks slot machine. But since that isn't going to happen in our lifetime, here's a list of other things you can see for free. (These can change, so no lawsuits, please.)

1) The best free attraction in Vegas is the **sea battle at Treasure Island** between a British frigate and a good old pirate ship. Every 90 minutes after 4 p.m. (Watch from across the street where it's not so crowded.)

2) See the spectacular **Fountains of Bellagio** (1,100 fountains, 20 million gallons of water) on the eight-acre lake fronting the hotel. The water sways and sprays as high as 240 feet every 30 minutes. Special treat is watching owner Kirk Kerkorian snorkel for coins on the lake's bottom.

3) Want to feel the world shake and the heavens roar? Have a couple of piña coladas at the **Lagoon Saloon inside the Mirage**. Next best would be the free volcano eruption outside the Mirage—every 15 minutes from dusk to midnight, weather permitting.

4) Visit **Masquerade Village at the Rio**, and watch the Masquerade Show in the Sky—an interactive extravaganza where onlookers can wear costumes and take part in a parade of sky floats on an overhead track looking down on the casino. It's New Orleans like New Orleans oughta be. Every other hour throughout most of the day and evening.

5) The Forum Shops at Caesars Palace are a must-see on your Vegas vacation. It'll cost you if you go inside the stores, but no more than it would in a regular mall. There are two fountain shows at the Forum Shops: Festival Fountain and Atlantis. Both come to life every hour on the hour, and both are free. Get there 15 minutes early for the best spot.

6) The Fremont Street Experience is a light and sound show unlike any you've ever seen. Programmed by 32 computers (run by a 17-year-old named Rick), over two million lights create vivid animated images synchronized with music and sound under a five-block canopy. The seven-minute show starts every hour on the hour, beginning at dusk.

7) See the **Antique and Classic Auto Collection at the Imperial Palace**, a display of over 200 rare old automobiles. Normally, tickets are $6.95 for this attraction, but Imperial Palace gives away tickets to anyone who asks for them. The auto collection is hard to find, but just take the elevator at the rear of the casino to the 5th floor of the parking garage. Don't get off on the 6th floor. There are more antique cars here, but these belong to the employees.

8) The Bellagio Conservatory features over a thousand bins of exotic plants and flowers (changed seasonally) under a huge glass dome. That long line of people isn't waiting to see the flowers. They're getting treated for bee stings.

9) See the **Lion Habitat at the MGM Grand**, a four-level cave you can walk through—with ferocious lions just out of reach through a real thin pane of Plexiglas. The tour is free, but a picture with the animals will set you back $20.

10) For a bit of culture, see the **statue of David in the Appian Way shopping arcade at Caesars Palace.** The statue is the same size as the original by Michelangelo. Popular photo by tourists here is standing 25 feet in front of the statue, then holding out one hand as if cradling David's private parts. Is this crudity at its height, or what? (Although the five rolls of film I took came out pretty good.)

Honorable Mention: The Wildlife Walk at the Tropicana (inside the covered walkway between the Trop's twin towers) gives you a bird's eye view of the gardens and pool area, as well as a closeup peek at some lovable boa constrictors and pythons.

The Elvis Collection at the Las Vegas Hilton displays a jumpsuit worn by Elvis, a guitar played by Elvis, and a bronze statue of Elvis. Where's it located? Well, it's down at the end of Lonely Street at Heartbreak Hotel . . . or near the lobby.

There's a **battle between a fire-eating dragon and Merlin the Magician** every hour on the hour in front of the Excalibur. Guess who wins?

Check out the **display of gold nuggets at the Golden Nugget**, including a 61-pound chunk of pure gold called the "Hand of Faith." (I'd believe, too, if I had 61 pounds of gold in my pocket.)

Where can I take the kids?

How about their grandma's house? But if they're already here, then drop 'em off (with adult supervision) at

Circus Circus, Grand Slam Canyon, Luxor's Virtualand, Wet 'n' Wild, Excalibur's Magic Motion rides, or the Lied Discovery Children's Museum—which is the fourth largest children's museum in the world.

Are there any other museums in Las Vegas?

There's the Nevada State Museum at Lorenzi Park, the UNLV Museum on the campus of the University of Nevada Las Vegas, the Natural History Museum on Las Vegas Boulevard North, the Guggenheim Hermitage Museum at the Venetian, the Liberace Museum on East Tropicana, the Magic & Movie Hall of Fame at O'Sheas, Madame Tussaud's Celebrity Encounter (wax museum) at the Venetian, the Guinness World of Records Museum on Las Vegas Boulevard South, and the Elvis-a-Rama Museum with more than $3 million worth of Elvis memorabilia at 3401 Industrial Road.

The best museum in Southern Nevada is the Lost City Museum, 60 miles northeast of Vegas at Overton. Exhibits include a full-scale reconstruction of an Indian pueblo, which shows what Las Vegas looked like before Steve Wynn was born.

What is that big Coca Cola bottle on the Strip?

It's a $94 million shopping arcade called "The Showcase." Coca Cola is one of the tenants, with a 12,000 square foot retail and entertainment complex including a great old fashioned soda fountain. In fact, that Coke bottle you see outside is 150 feet high and houses two elevators! Now if they just had a 150-foot bourbon bottle next to it, I'd never go home.

Other attractions include M&M's World, GameWorks, and an eight-plex movie theater.

What is the largest hotel in Las Vegas?

The MGM Grand has 5,005 rooms, and that makes it the second-largest hotel in the world. (Some joint in

Thailand is number one with 5,100 rooms.) The other eight largest hotels in the world are all in Las Vegas. In order, Luxor (4,407 rooms), Mandalay Bay (3,700 rooms and 500 suites), Excalibur (4,032 rooms), Flamingo Hilton (3,642 rooms), Las Vegas Hilton (3,174 rooms), Mirage (3,049 rooms), Venetian (3,036 suites), and Monte Carlo (3,014 rooms).

What is the largest hotel in Atlantic City?

Who cares?

What is the smallest hotel in Las Vegas?

The Golden Gate, with 106 rooms.

How many hotel rooms are there in Las Vegas?

At last report, there were approximately 130,000 hotel rooms in the city—and for some reason most of them are on the 22nd floor and 150 yards from the elevator.

What is a concierge?

Back in the days of Julius Caesar, a concierge was a slave. Then it became a sort of servant: *con* (with) *cierge* (service). In a casino, the concierge is the intermediary between the guest and the hotel. It's a heck of an idea and was instituted in Las Vegas by Caesars Palace in late 1996. Now almost half the resorts in town utilize the services of a concierge.

Here's how one concierge explained her job. "We order flowers and gifts. We arrange dinner and show reservations inside and outside the hotel, limousine service, even shopping tours and weddings. We try to provide all the services needed by the hotel guest."

And if you're not a guest of the hotel? "We still help them. Of course, we're going to help our guests first."

What's the most unusual request she ever received? "One time we had a woman who was going to get married, and she didn't want to go shopping. So her fiancé gave me the money, and I bought her a wedding dress, hose, shoes, makeup . . . everything she would need to get married in."

Another concierge says he reads the business sections of five newspapers each morning. "One of my customers may have received a promotion and I want to be among the first to offer congratulations." He says a good concierge can turn guest requests into special experiences. "I can get you and your wife reservations in a popular restaurant, but I'd rather send you to a little out-of-the-way place with great food and real atmosphere. Better yet, I can arrange a romantic picnic on a quiet spot overlooking the city." Yeah, but if I wanted to eat a sandwich on the side of a mountain, why would I need a concierge?

(For hotels without the services of a concierge, use V.I.P. Services.)

What is the proper amount to tip a concierge?

Anywhere from $5 to $20, and more if they make miracles happen.

What is a marker?

A marker is an IOU from U to I, only in this case I is the casino. (See chart.) In order to get a marker in a casino, you must have a line of credit at the casino cage. You can do this by setting up a credit line through your hometown bank, or by making a cash deposit when you arrive at the hotel. If you're like me, you hate to walk around with $200,000 in your wallet. It's dangerous, and it's downright uncomfortable. Simply deposit the money at the cage, and then every time you gamble you can take some of your money back in the form of a marker.

The nice thing about taking markers is that everyone thinks you're a high roller, including the casino personnel.

Markers Issued in the Pit

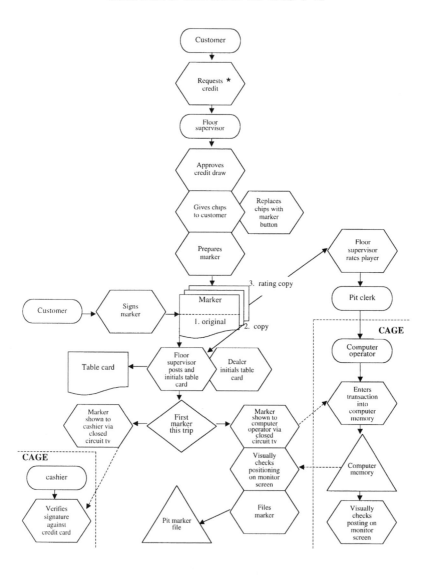

*assumes that the customer has previously established a line of credit

You'll be treated royally and lavished with all kinds of casino amenities—until your money runs out. But think of the wonderful memories you'll have on the bus ride back home.

"Because of the computer, everything we do today is based on what a person's play shows. This has been a little difficult for some of the older players because years ago we didn't really know if they were playing or not. Now, we simply check the computer to see how much they're playing and the length of time they're playing. Both these things reflect on their rating as a player. I can't argue with this system because the computers are right. This is a business which has to show a profit and this is one way to do it."

Tropicana Host

What is a rating slip?

Any player who bets a large sum of money or any player that has taken a marker will be rated by the floor supervisor while he plays. Information on the rating slip includes the player's buy-in, his length of time at the table, and his average bet. When the player leaves the table, the supervisor will also note how much money the player won or lost. This way, if the player asks for any casino complimentaries, his play has been recorded, and the casino knows at a glance how much to offer him in the way of comps.

Comps are based on three factors: average bet, the length of time at the game, and the game's house edge. These three numbers are calculated to arrive at the casino's "theoretical win." Generally, the casino is willing to give back 25 to 40% of that amount in comps. In other words, they'll give you back up to half of what they expect to win from you.

Comps are the casino's way of thanking you for getting dry-cleaned there instead of somewhere else. In one recent year, the Atlantic City casino industry passed out almost $740 million in comps out of a gross revenue of $3 billion. A lot of people get comps, and so can you.

In order to get a comp, though, you usually have to be rated. Simply give your name to the supervisor when you come to the table. You'll be rated just like the high rollers are, and entitled to the same special treatment. In addition, the casino will know who to bill when you throw your chair through the plate glass window after losing your life savings.

> *"I'd advise customers to open a credit line at the casino. It makes the casino aware of what you're willing to risk. And if we know what you're willing to risk, then that formulates in our mind what we could extend to you in comps."*
>
> Las Vegas Casino Manager

Can I get comps by playing the slot machines?

Yes, although comps for slot players are usually tighter because of slot club cashbacks or merchandise giveaways. Of course, it doesn't hurt to try, so be sure to give your name to a slot host before cranking those handles. Remember, though, that if you have to gamble $300 to $500 a hand for four hours to get a room, food and beverages, limo service and use of the hotel spa (Gold River Casino comp guideline), how long would you have to play a 25¢ slot machine to get the same perks?

How do I know what comps I'm entitled to?

Call the hotel beforehand and ask for a host. Tell him you're interested in playing at his casino, and ask him what it takes to get a free room, RFB (room, food, beverages), or free air fare. He'll tell you how much you have to bet, and how many hours a day you have to play to get any of these.

If he tells you that you have to bet $50 a hand for four hours to get a free room, don't let that scare you off. You could bet $25 a hand for eight hours, and be entitled to the same thing. Remember, though, that you have to gamble in order to get room and RFB comps, and most of the time it's cheaper just to pay for it.

Is there any other way to get a comp?

It's fairly easy to get a comp to the buffet because it's usually the cheapest—for you and the casino. A breakfast buffet may cost you $3.95, but it costs the casino about 60¢. It's also easier to get a comp in a large casino, because smaller casinos work on a lower profit margin.

Don't be afraid to ask. Getting something for nothing is what put Vegas on the map in the first place. Here's how one fellow did it. "Can I get a comp?" he asked the pit boss.

"A comp to what?"

"Anything!"

What if I ask for a comp to the coffee shop and get the buffet instead?

Take it. You're getting something for nothing, remember? Never turn down a comp! Here's what can happen. A man was playing blackjack in a ritzy casino: $10 a pop but sitting out one of every three hands. He played for 15 minutes, then asked the supervisor for a meal. His action didn't warrant anything (10 hands at $10 divided by a theoretical win of 2 percent = $2), but the supervisor offered him a comp to the buffet. Well, the man didn't want the buffet. "The food's terrible," he complained. "How about the gourmet restaurant?"

"I can't do that," the supervisor said. "But I can put you in the coffee shop."

"No, I don't like the food in there, either."

The outcome was that the man didn't get anything. So again, repeat after me: Never turn down a comp.

Where's the easiest place to get a comp?

These figures from the Gaming Control Board's Gaming Abstract sum it up pretty well.

Downtown Las Vegas: 72% of the drinks, 38% of the meals, and 30% of the rooms are comped.

The Strip: 46% of the drinks, 18% of the meals, and 14% of the rooms are comped.

Laughlin: 70% of the drinks, 22% of the meals, and 18% of the rooms are comped.

Statewide, comps (including fight and show tickets and air fares for good customers) cost casino resorts over $1 billion a year!

What can I get if I don't gamble?

Not much. At one time it was fairly easy to get souvenir cards from the casino. Nowadays, though, most casinos deal cards from multiple-deck shoes, and it takes too many man hours to sort the cards back into individual decks. If you do manage to get a free deck of cards, there'll be a hole punched in the middle of the deck or the corners will be lopped off (in order to prevent them from being slipped into a real game).

Your best bet is to ask for some souvenir dice; they're changed on each table every eight hours. If all else fails, ask for a gaming guide. These make wonderful souvenirs, and they're free. Another great "freebie" are the sturdy plastic change cups that are yours for the taking in every casino. Pick up one at each club you visit, and now you've got a great little memento of your Vegas vacation.

The only other free things I can think of are parking validation and cocktails. Many casinos are even strict about drinks, so sit down at a slot machine until a cocktail waitress walks by. She doesn't know whether you're playing or not, and she doesn't care. She's after a tip, so give her a big smile and get a dollar out. If there's more than one in your party, you'll really be money ahead.

What is the oldest living thing in Nevada?

It's a tie between the bristlecone pine tree (4,000 years old) and a cocktail waitress named Big Bertha at the El Cortez.

What if I lose something in the casino?

If you lose money, chalk it off as one of life's little disappointments. Nobody turns in cash, chips, or cups of coins. But people are pretty good about returning other things: cameras, video recorders, purses, wallets, checkbooks, glasses, binoculars, umbrellas, jackets, medicine, car keys, pipes, magazines, canes, strollers, shoes, rings, watches, bracelets, necklaces, attaché cases. Just check at the security desk, but be prepared to describe the lost article right down to the color of her eyes.

Casino porters find a lot of stuff. One told me he found a shopping bag crammed with $18,000 worth of French francs. The porter turned the bag over to securi-

---

TIP FROM A LAS VEGAS PORTER: *"If you find an empty cigarette box in a casino, look inside it before you throw it away. A lot of people keep cash and casino chips inside a cigarette box. Sometimes you'll even find money tucked inside the cellophane wrapper on a cigarette package."*

ty, where somebody later claimed it and didn't even tip the porter. On the other hand, the same porter once turned in an empty purse and got a $5 reward.

Can I get my own private game in a casino?

Private games are strictly for high rollers, so don't ask for one unless you're a sheik, prince, movie star . . . or former governor of Louisiana.

Can I watch a game in a casino without playing?

Sure. In fact, it's fun. At the dice table you may be asked to make room for someone who wants to play, but if it's quiet no one will mind. At baccarat, stay behind the velvet ropes. At other games, stand behind the players so that you're not in the way. If by chance you happen to be watching some high roller who wants privacy, his eight-foot bodyguard will tell you. Otherwise, watch as long as you want—and think of all the money you're saving.

How do I buy chips in a casino?

You can buy them at the cashier's cage, or at the table where you plan to play. Simply place your money on the table in front of you, and ask for change. Never put your money in the betting circle of a game. The dealer might think it's a bet. That's why it's always a good idea to tell the dealer you want change. It isn't necessary to specify the denomination of chips when you get change. If the minimum bet at the table is $5, the dealer will give you $5 chips.

One dealer related the following story. A man dropped a $100 bill on the table and said, "Give me twenty-five dollar chips." So the dealer gave him 25 $1 chips and three $25 chips.

"No," the man said. "Give me twenty-five dollar chips." This time the dealer gave him four $25 chips.

"No," the man said. "Give me twenty-five dollar

chips." What the man wanted was 20 $5 chips, which is what he would have gotten if he hadn't said anything.

On another game, a player dropped a $100 bill on the table. "Give me twenty ones," he said to the dealer.

The dealer, who was in the process of shuffling the cards, smiled and said, "I'll try."

After the shuffle was completed, she gave the man twenty $5 chips.

"Give me twenty ones," he repeated.

"I'll try," she smiled again. Well, of course, she thought the man wanted her to deal him a 21 on every hand, and what he wanted was twenty $1 chips.

Can I take chips from one casino to another?

Technically, chips are only negotiable at the casino where you buy them. If you're a known player, or if you only have a couple of foreign chips, take them to the cashier's cage. The cage will usually accept them.

To be on the safe side, convert your chips into currency before you leave. To make it easier for you to carry the chips to the cage, "color up" at the table before leaving. That means changing all your $1 and $5 chips into $25 chips—or (hopefully) $100 chips.

Can I use chips to pay for meals or drinks in the casino?

No. Chips can only be used at the games, or for tips.

How much does the casino pay for slot machines and other gambling equipment?

Electronic slot machines cost around $5,000, which doesn't include the gaming taxes paid every year on each one. Dice cost $2.50 a pair, and they're usually changed three times a day. Playing cards are around $1 a pack, and the casino orders them in 60,000 to 100,000-deck lots.

Gaming chips, made of a plastic/clay composition, cost around 45¢ apiece.

Where did playing cards originate?

Nobody knows for sure, but the most popular theory is that wandering gypsies first used cards to tell fortunes. Afterwards, you'd get a "club" in the "heart" with a "spade" for your "diamonds."

The following question was worth $250,000 on a national quiz show.

On which two card suits are the one-eyed jacks displayed?

      (A) Spades and diamonds
      (B) Spades and hearts
      (C) Clubs and diamonds
      (D) Hearts and clubs

The answer is at the bottom of the page. By the way, don't feel bad if you don't know the answer. I didn't get it right, either, and neither did any of the blackjack supervisors where I work.

Why do so many wealthy people gamble?

A dealer once posed this same question to a man in his thirties who was betting $100,000 a hand at baccarat. Here was the man's answer:

"When I'm at home, my whole day is planned. I know where I'm having lunch, I know which business deals I'm going to close. If I want to buy a new car, I make a phone call. They bring over a fleet of them and I pick the one I want. If I want to buy a new house, I call my real estate

The answer to the $250,000 question is: (B) Spades and hearts agent and she takes care of it. There's really no anticipation in my life.

"But when I'm at the baccarat tables, I don't know what the next card is going to be. I don't know if I'm going to win or not. Gambling is the one challenge I have not been able to master."

You might want to use this line the next time you're on your psychiatrist's couch.

1
The Good, the Bad, and the Ugly

I've seen a lot of new games in the casino. Are they popular?

Some are; some aren't. **Caribbean Stud** is probably the most popular of these so-called carnival games. You make an ante, you're dealt five cards, you double your ante if you're happy with your hand, and then you try to beat the dealer's hand. Drawback: If the dealer does not qualify by having at least an ace and a king, the game is over and you're only paid for your original ante. (The dealer will only qualify about 55% of the time.)

A popular side bet at this game is betting an additional dollar to win a progressive jackpot. Betting the extra dollar is not a good idea, even if the jackpot gets up to $200,000. Odds of drawing a royal flush on your first five cards are almost 650,000-1.

At Caribbean Stud, here's your basic strategy in a nutshell: Call the dealer if your five-card hand is ace-king-jack-8-3 or better. Fold otherwise. This way you've given yourself a chance to win, even if the dealer qualifies. That's all there is to it.

Let It Ride is unique, because you're not playing against the dealer or any other player. You're just trying to make a good poker hand. Each player makes three separate bets. The dealer then deals each player three cards. If you're not happy with the cards you're dealt, take back your first bet by scratching your cards on the table. If you like your hand so far, let it ride! The dealer then deals one community card face up. Bad card? Take back your second bet. Good card? Let it ride! Now one more community card face up. This time you've gotta stay. And the better your hand, the more you win.

Staying in the game with all three bets is not advisable if you don't have at least a pair of 10s—which is the lowest winning hand. Having three high cards isn't much better, unless you can use them in a straight flush or a royal. Expect to stay in the game with all three bets about once every 16 hands.

There's also an illuminated side bet which pays you extra for a straight or better. This is called the "tournament" spot, and it costs an extra $1 per hand. All payouts are in addition to your regular Let It Ride awards, and can be as high as $20,000 for that elusive royal flush. Again, though, remember the odds: 650,000-1.

Three-Card Poker is being hailed as the next big game in Vegas. The player gets three cards; the dealer gets three cards. In this game, there are several betting options. You can play "pair-plus," where you're simply trying to make a good three-card poker hand. A pair pays even money, a three-card flush pays 4-1, a straight 6-1, three-of-a-kind 30-1, and a three-card straight flush pays 40-1.

Or you can make an ante and play the dealer heads-up, making an equal bet on the "play" spot if you think you've got the dealer beat. Dealer must qualify by having at least a queen high, otherwise the player only gets paid for his ante. The only variance from regular poker is that in three-card poker a straight beats a flush. Most people play both hands, because if you lose the "pair-plus" hand you've got a chance to get your money back by taking on the dealer. Stanley Ko, in his booklet *Mastering the Game of Three-Card Poker*, recommends making the "play" wager only if you hold a queen-6-4 hand or better.

House edge on the "pair-plus" bet is 2.3%; house edge on the ante bet is 2.1%.

Another new game is **Vegas Shootout**. You make up to three separate bets of equal amounts in circles marked "Royal Match," "2 Card Poker," and "5 Card Poker." You're dealt two cards and the dealer gets three, the last one face down. (There's one joker that can be used as a wild card.) If your two cards are a flush you get paid 2-1 in the "Royal Match" circle, and 15-1 if your first two cards are a same-suited king and queen without the joker. No flush? Then you lose your bet. If you have a higher ranking poker hand than the dealer's first two cards, you win even money in the "2 Card Poker" circle. The dealer's third card is then turned over, and now you're using all the cards at "5 Card Poker." Payoffs here range from even money for a pair of jacks to 5,000-1 for a royal flush (no joker).

Your best bet is "2 Card Poker," because the house has no edge over you. Disadvantage: You have to bet on at least one of the other two options. The house edge on this game, though, is only 2.8%. Broken down, it's 3.9% on the "Royal Match" bet, dead even on the two-card showdown, and 4.6% on the five-card hand.

The granddaddy of casino poker games is **Pai Gow Poker**. You're dealt seven cards, and you make two poker hands out of them: five cards in your highest hand, two in your second highest hand. The object of the game is to beat the banker's two hands with your two hands. If you do, you win your bet. If you don't, you lose. Win one hand and lose one hand, and it's a push. The casino makes its money at this game by charging you a 5% commission when you win both bets.

This game takes about 20 minutes to learn, and it's my personal favorite because almost half the hands end in a push. Since no money changes hands on a push, you can play a long time on a limited bankroll.

What happens if you set your hands wrong at pai gow or pai gow poker?

If your second highest hand is higher than your highest hand, it's called a foul hand and you could forfeit your bet. Most casinos are fairly lax about enforcing this rule, however, so if you set your hands wrong just shrug and say you're sorry.

One of the nice things about these games is that if you're not sure how to set your hands, the dealer will do it for you!

What is the difference between pai gow and pai gow poker?

Pai gow is an ancient Asian game played with tiles, while pai gow poker is played with an ordinary deck of 52 cards plus one joker (which can be used as an ace or to complete a straight or flush). Pai gow poker is much easier to learn, and consequently easier to play.

What is "fortune" pai gow poker?

This is an optional bet that you make in addition to your regular wager which offers bonus payoffs for special hands. All seven cards are used to qualify for a "fortune" bonus, and payoffs can be as high as 8,000-1 for a seven-card straight flush (without the joker).

You can also qualify for an "envy bonus" by betting at least $5 in the fortune circle. If another player draws a winning hand (anything from four-of-a-kind to a seven-card straight flush), you receive an envy bonus of up to $5,000!

BEWARE. If you play fortune pai gow poker, look for a no limit table. Otherwise, there's an aggregate payout and you may not win the full amount.

Which casino games are pure luck, and which ones require skill?

Games of luck include the Big 6, baccarat, keno, reel-type slots, and roulette. Games requiring some skill are craps, blackjack, pai gow poker, Caribbean Stud, Let It Ride, video poker, and regular poker. Of course, there will always be an element of luck in any casino game, so it never hurts to pray before you play.

What is Casino War?

Based on the childhood game of "battle," the dealer gives you a card and then he takes a card. High card wins. It's about as exciting as a Wendy's commercial, and it's geared toward the player who can't figure out how to play blackjack or any other game in the casino. The drawback comes when your card ties the dealer's card. In that case, you either go to war with the dealer by doubling your bet and getting one more card, or surrendering and forfeiting half your bet. If you tie the dealer again after going to war, you automatically win.

But here's where the casino has the edge. If you win after going to war, you only get paid for your original bet. If you lose after going to war, you lose both bets. Hey, those Wendy's commercials are looking better all the time!

What are the best games to play in the casino?

Video poker, baccarat, craps, and basic strategy blackjack. I call them the "big four," because all four of these games have a house edge (or advantage) of 1% or less.

1) Video Poker: Slot machines that let you decide whether you win or not. The best of the bunch is full-pay deuces wild, which offers a payback of 100.7% long-term when you use optimum strategy. A royal flush pays $1,000 (when maximum quarters are played), and 4 deuces gives you a nice secondary jackpot of $250. The strategy is simple. On the deal, keep deuces, any three cards to a royal flush, any four cards to a straight or flush, three-of-a-kind, or a pair.

Drawback: Anything under a royal flush pays less than other video poker machines.

Always check the awards glass before playing any video poker machine. At deuces wild, some machines only pay 4 coins (per coin played) for 4-of-a-kind. Full pay machines pay 5 coins (per coin played) for 4-of-a-kind. It doesn't sound like a big difference, but it changes your overall payback from 100.7% to 94.3%!

---

2) Blackjack: The most popular table game in the casino, but played incorrectly by most novice players. The house edge at blackjack, or "21" as casinos call it, is 2%, but only 0.06% if you use optimum basic strategy. Using basic strategy, always assume the dealer's hole card is a 10—because there are more 10s in the deck than anything else.

STAND if you've got a total of 12 or more and the dealer is showing a bad card (2, 3, 4, 5, or 6). Exception: Hit a 12 if the dealer is showing a 2 or 3. **HIT** If you've got a total of 16 or less and the dealing is showing a good card (7, 8, 9, 10, or ace). Basic strategy isn't foolproof, but it does lower the house edge to under 1%. Why? Because you're playing the same way consistently. The dealer plays the same way every hand, and so should you.

Other key strategies at blackjack:

• **Always split aces and 8s.** Match your original bet and make two hands out of one hand. See the detailed chart in the blackjack chapter on splitting other pairs.

• **Double down with 11 unless the dealer is showing an ace.** Match your original bet (or any thing up to it) and get one more card. Double down with 9 or an ace and any small card unless the dealer is showing a 10 or an ace. Double down with 9 or an ace and any small card (2 through 7) if the dealer is showing a 5 or 6.

A young man attended a blackjack class in a Vegas casino, frantically trying to remember everything the instructor told him. Don't take insurance. Double down with 11. Always split aces and 8s. Then he went to a real game, and after several hands was dealt an ace and 8. He immediately doubled his bet. "What are you doing?" the dealer asked him. "I'm splitting," he announced proudly. "My instructor told me to always split aces and 8s."

---

3) Baccarat: Strictly a game of chance where you're guessing which hand will be closest to 9—the player's hand or the banker's hand. (You're not the player and the house isn't the banker; those are just the names of the hands.) Aces count as one, 10s and face cards as 0, and 2s through 9s at face value. Two cards are dealt to both player and banker. Only the last digit counts, so if player has a 9 and 4, the total is 3. Player takes a third and final card with a total of less than 6. Exception: If the first two cards by either player or banker add up to 8 or 9, it's called a "natural," and no more cards are dealt.

Banker will win slightly more than half the hands (because player's cards are turned over first and this sometimes determines whether banker will take a third card), so a 5% commission is charged on winning bank bets. The house edge is around 1% no matter which hand you bet (banker 1.06%, player 1.24%).

Mini-Baccarat is the same game, only the mini-version is played at a regular table in the regular casino with regular people just like you. Table limits are usually lower, winning commissions are paid after each hand, and the dealer deals the cards so the game goes faster. Also gaining popularity is midi-baccarat, with seating positions for five players: numbers one, two, three, five, and six. (Four is considered an unlucky number in Asia.) Same rules apply, except each player gets a turn dealing the cards, the table minimums are usually higher than at mini-baccarat, and new cards are used after each shoe.

4) Craps: The most exciting game in the casino, and also the most confusing. The complicated layout is enough to scare even Indiana Jones, but keep in mind that both sides of the layout are the same, and the battery of bets in the middle of the table are all long-shots. Your best bet at this game is the pass line, where you're betting the shooter will roll a winner. Seven or 11 wins on the first roll. Two, 3, and 12 lose on the first roll. (These are known as craps, which is where the game got its name.) Any other number becomes the point, and the shooter must roll that number again before rolling another 7. Once the shooter has a point number (4, 5, 6, 8, 9, or 10), then take odds by placing an additional bet behind your wager on the pass line. By taking odds, you're getting the true payoff for that number, giving the casino no advantage over you for your odds bet.

Equally as good is a come bet, where your bet "comes" to the next number that rolls, and then taking odds on that bet as well. Most experts agree that a bet on the pass line with the odds and two come bets with the odds is the wise way to play, giving the house an advantage of 1.41% for your pass line and come bets and only

0.8% for single odds. There are only six point numbers, and by making three bets you've covered half of them! Stay away from the proposition bets; the house edge on these can climb as high as 17%.

What is the house edge at other casino games?

In order, they are pai gow and pai gow poker 2.5%, single zero roulette 2.6%, Vegas Shootout 2.8%, $1 reel slots 3%, Casino War 3.5%, Let It Ride 3.5%, double zero roulette 5.2%, Caribbean Stud 5.3%, 25¢ reel slots 8%, 5¢ reel slots 15%, the Big 6 18%, and keno up to 30%.

What is the casino's most profitable game?

Casinos generate up to 70% of their revenue from slot machines. Other money-makers for the casino include a "hold" or profit of around 25% at roulette, 18% at baccarat, 15% at craps, and 14% at blackjack.

How much profit does a slot machine generate each year?

On average, about $30,000. This compares with around $600,000 for each table game.

Here's an example of how important slot machines are to the overall success of a casino operation. In one Strip casino, an area was cleared of a brass stairway in preparation for a large remodeling job. Electricians, carpet layers, upholsterers, carpenters, and slot mechanics worked around the clock for three days to install a bank of 60 slot machines. Two weeks later, the machines were removed and the remodeling job continued. When asked why the casino went to all the trouble and expense of installing the machines for such a short period of time, the slot manager shrugged and said, "Two weeks is a lot of down time in a casino." In other words, the machines paid for themselves—and for all that labor—in just two weeks time.

How much money does the Las Vegas gambling industry gross each month?

The average win is about $330 million a month, or $137,500 an hour! Remember, though, that out of that profit come operating expenses: employee salaries ($975) and owner salaries ($32.7 million).

How much money does the casino pay out in license fees?

A lot. There's the annual state license fee ($16,000 for 17 or more table games plus $200 for each game in excess of 16); quarterly county license fee ($25 to $50 monthly on each table game); quarterly state license fee ($20,300 for 36 or more table games plus $25 for each game over 35); annual slot machine tax ($250 on each machine, which is earmarked for state educational funds); quarterly county slot machine license fee ($10 monthly for each machine); state slot machine license fee ($20 per machine on 16 or more); plus 6% of all gross gaming revenue each month exceeding $134,000. Gaming is also taxed at the federal and local government levels.

Almost half the state's operating budget is derived from taxes on gambling.

How does the casino tabulate its profit?

On slot machines, the drop from each machine is collected daily (in some casinos every other day), then taken to the count room for what's called the hard count. After the coins are counted, they are re-rolled so they can be used again. The coin count is compared to the payout readings on each machine to ensure that each one is holding its programmed percentage. All winning jackpots are verified at this time.

The casino also takes an inventory of chips and markers on each table game, either once a day or at the end of each shift. This is called "taking the count." The drop box from each game is then transported to the casino count room for the soft count. Each box is opened, the money is counted bill by bill, and markers are cross-checked for accuracy.

The members of the count team enter their figures on a "working stiff sheet" (or daily statistical summary), which is then sent to data processing and the accounting department. This eventually finds its way into the casino's daily profit-and-loss statement, a copy of which is sent to each department head.

"We had a horrible year. We expected profits to increase 13%, and they only increased 8%—so we lost 5%."

Moe Dalitz, Desert Inn, 1967

What are the safest bets I can make in the casino?

The pass line with odds at craps; single zero roulette; player or banker at baccarat; full-pay video poker with maximum coins; basic strategy blackjack; taking or laying the point spread on your favorite sports team; and bingo— where the casino makes money not on the game but by keeping you in the casino between sessions.

What are the worst bets?

Parlays and teasers at the sports book; proposition bets at the dice table; keno; the Big 6; betting the extra dollar on the progressive jackpot at Caribbean Stud or Let It Ride; betting on a tie hand at baccarat or Casino War; the five-number bet at roulette (0, 00, 1, 2, 3); and nickel slot machines. Casinos generally keep around 15% of the "drop" on nickel machines compared to 3% on a dollar machine, and here's the reason why. Three percent of a dollar is 3¢; 15% of a nickel is less than 1¢. In order for the casino to make the same percentage on a nickel machine, it would have to hold 60%! At 15%, you're getting off easy.

A young lady walked up to a Big 6 wheel, which is the game where the dealer spins a big wheel and the players bet on where it's going to stop. The lady gave the dealer a $20 bill, and the dealer gave the lady $20 in chips. "Excuse me," the lady said with a frown. "Don't I get darts?" She thought it was a spinning dart game! Well, I shouldn't laugh. That'll probably be the next big game in Vegas.

I saw an $8 chip at the Luxor. What gives?

The Luxor issued the $8 chip in honor of the Chinese New Year. (Eight is a lucky number in China.) You should have bought one. Chip collecting has become a profitable hobby, and an $8 chip is truly unique. Some gambling chips have really sky-rocketed in value, including the original $5 Desert Inn chip ($1,000), any chip from the Flamingo issued before owner Bugsy Siegel's death in 1947 ($6,000 to $9,000), a $25 chip from the El Rancho ($125), a 50¢ token from Caesars Palace ($12), and the $1 chip from the old S.S. Rex gambling ship ($375). Other good collectibles would be the George Burns chip from Caesars Palace, and chips of any denomination from the Dunes, Sands, Hacienda, or any other casino that closes.

Beware of casinos that issue commemorative chips at the drop of a hat. Remember, these chips are only costing the casinos about 45¢ apiece, and that's about all they'll ever be worth. Why would a casino issue so many commemorative chips? Unscramble the following letters to learn the casino's motive.

R   E   G   D   E

Can I bet cash at a table game or do I have to play with chips?

If you want to play with cash, go ahead. Just say "money plays" when you make your bet. If you win, though, you'll be paid with chips.

Can I make a call bet?

Most casinos allow you to make one call bet; i.e., you're allowed to call one bet without having money in evidence. If you win, you'll be paid the amount of your call bet. If you lose, start digging.

Should I bet more when I lose?

No, no, NO! As I explained in my other books (*Las Vegas Behind the Tables*, *Chip-Wrecked in Las Vegas*, *Gone With the Wind*, *A Tale of Two Cities*), only bet more when you're winning. Otherwise, why would the casino have table limits?

I once saw a player double up after losing a $5 bet. His next bet was $10, then $20, $40, $80, $160, $320, $640. He won the $640 bet, but what did he win? Five dollars! And to win it he invested a total of $1,275.

Be patient. Never double up to catch up. Manage your bankroll properly by using a money management system. The most popular of these is going up one unit every time you win, then going back to your initial bet when you lose. Another popular strategy is "plateau" betting, where you make the same bet for three winning hands, then begin a double-up system starting with a 5-unit bet.

What is the most dangerous pitfall for a gambler?

I would say it's those last couple of hours before your plane leaves. You're stuck, you're mad, you want one last chance to win all your money back. Don't fall into this trap. You're not going to win every time you play, and the key is never to lose more than you can afford.

What else should I be wary of doing?

Drinking too much while you gamble, playing while you're tired or sleepy, and gambling at any game without full knowledge of all the options that are available. This is particularly true at blackjack. In some casinos, you can only double down with 10 or 11. Other casinos won't let you double down after you split pairs.

At the dice tables, most casinos offer you a chance to take more than even odds on your pass line and come bets. Some casinos (Caesars Palace, for one) don't charge you a commission on "buy" or "lay" bets until you win. This lowers the house edge even more. Always check your options before playing.

Why does the dealer clap his hands when he leaves the table?

Because he's so %$#@ happy to be leaving! No, it's casino procedure for the dealer to clear his hands before leaving the table. This shows the supervisor that the dealer has nothing up his sleeve, so to speak.

When a blackjack dealer receives a tip, you'll also notice that he taps the chip on the table before putting it in his shirt pocket. This is to alert the supervisor that he is taking money off the game.

What should I do if the dealer makes a mistake while I'm playing?

If it's in your favor, don't do anything. If it's going to cost you money, stop the game! I've seen blackjack dealers forget to deal themselves a hand, and dealers who dealt themselves the "cut" card without even noticing it. I've seen crap tables where five was marked as the point on one end, and eight as the point on the other end. I've seen stickmen give the dice to the wrong shooter! Here comes a loser 7, and then this tiny voice: "Hey, I thought I was shooting!" In cases like this, scream to high heaven. You'll usually get your money back. Of course, the dealer will hate you for making him look bad, so gather up all your ill-gotten gains and head for the next table.

A word of caution: If a dealer overpays a player, he can put his job in jeopardy. At the MGM Grand, a famous former baseball player (whose last name is the same as a popular flower) was overpaid $20,000 when the dealer converted all his chips into larger ones. The mistake wasn't noticed until later that day, at which time one of the casino bosses went to the player's room and asked him to give the money back. The player refused, and as a result the dealer and supervisor were fired.

What's the most money you ever saw anyone win in a casino?

A short Asian man with a thin moustache won $8 million playing baccarat in a Las Vegas casino. Of course, he was betting $250,000 a hand, and in a case like that it doesn't take long to win or lose a large sum of money.

One thing I've noticed is that people who holler the loudest while they're gambling are usually those betting the least amount of money. Actor Telly Savalas would only accept $5 chips when he gambled in a casino. He would bet large stacks of $5 chips, and a crowd always gathered around the table. They weren't watching because he was Telly Savalas. They were watching because they thought he was a betting a lot more money than he really was.

Most bonafide high rollers prefer gambling in their own private casinos, and just about every Vegas resort has a separate gaming parlor set aside for these whales (as they are called in casino jargon). Here they can gamble to their heart's content, and afterwards eat and drink to their heart's content in the private dining salon next to the private powder room behind the private gaming parlor.

Another way that casinos attract high rollers is with banks of $100 and $500 slot machines. These haven't done so well, because the smallest jackpot on a $500 machine is $2,500. Every time a player hits one of these jackpots, he has to stop playing and fill out a tax form.

Here's another way to keep the masses from knowing how much is being wagered at the tables. Some high rollers will play with regular casino chips, only each of their chips could be worth as much as $25,000. Even though the person next to you is betting the same color chip as you, he might be betting much more—and now you'll never know for sure.

Speaking of high rollers, here's a story I blatantly lifted right out of Anthony Curtis' *Las Vegas Advisor*. Australian billionaire Kerry Packer was playing in the private gaming salon at Bellagio, and became annoyed by an Asian player who hollered every time he won and every time he lost. Packer approached the man and asked him to tone it down. The gambler became irate, pounded the table, and shouted, "Do you know who I am? I'm worth forty million dollars." Packer stood there for a moment, then said, "Tell you what . . . I'll flip you for it."

What is the most money you ever saw anyone lose?

Eight million dollars at baccarat, by a short Asian man with a thin moustache.

However, the biggest riches to rags story is a man who's been a fixture in Vegas baccarat rooms since 1978. In that period of time, he's lost an astounding $78 million!

In a plush Vegas casino, a wealthy gambler lost $2 million in one day at the crap table. He chuckled as he signed the marker. "I made $15 million today in the stock market." Kind of hard to feel sorry for him, isn't it?

What is the most money you ever saw anyone tip a dealer?

To answer your question in a dramatic fashion, let me set the scene for you. An Australian gambler (Kerry Packer again) was playing blackjack, betting all six spots on the table at $25,000 a hand. After eight hours, he decided to quit. He tossed his remaining seven chips to the dealer. "That's for you," he said. Each chip was worth $25,000, resulting in a tip of $175,000! Unfortunately, the dealer had to split her tips with all the other blackjack dealers, but it sure made her popular that night.

Packer once left a table with a large handful of chips. He noticed a few pink chips scattered amongst his $25,000 chips. "What are these?" he asked a pit boss.

"Those are $500 chips," the pit boss answered.

"How did I get them?" the Australian asked.

"On your blackjacks," the pit boss explained patiently. "Every time you got a blackjack the dealer paid you an extra $12,500."

"Well, I don't want those," the Australian frowned. At that moment a cocktail waitress walked past, holding an empty tray. "Here you go, hon," the Australian said, and then he dropped all those $500 chips right on top of her tray.

What's the most bizarre thing that ever happened in a casino?

Here's my favorite. Sherlock Feldman was a crusty little pit boss at the old Dunes Hotel. One day he was watching a crap game when a man making a bet accidentally dropped his false teeth on the table. Sherlock popped out his own false teeth, laid them next to the other man's choppers, and growled, "You're faded!"

Is it true that casinos pump pure oxygen into the air to loosen a gambler's inhibitions?

This old chestnut has been floating around Vegas ever since Mario Puzo wrote about it in one of his books. It's not true, and neither is the rumor that the casino pumps certain scents into the hotel to lure you inside. What you feel when you enter a casino is—adrenaline. That's all.

What should I know about etiquette in the casino?

First of all, never touch your bet once a game starts. The moment you make your bet it isn't your money any longer. It's in limbo until the game is over. If your chips are crooked or fall over, don't worry about it. The dealer will straighten or stack them again. Don't count your chips if you decide to increase your bet at blackjack by splitting or doubling down. Let the dealer do it. To get change at the game, place your money on the table outside the betting circle. Dealers are not allowed to take money from your hand. Now let's go over the games one by one:

Blackjack: Use hand signals when you play. Where cards are dealt face down, tuck your cards under your bet if you don't want a card; scrape your cards lightly on the table if you do. Where cards are dealt face up, wave your hand behind your bet if you don't want a card; scratch the table with your finger if you do. If you wish to double down or split pairs, place your additional bet next to your original bet. Never cap your first bet with another one.

Don't give advice to other players. They won't listen anyway. By the same token, ignore unwanted advice from other players. They'll usually tell you what to do, whether you ask them or not.

Some blackjack players get upset if you enter the

game in the middle of the shoe. They've won six hands in a row, and now *you* sat down and ruined everything. Not true, of course, but it's good manners to ask the other players if you can join in.

Most novices avoid sitting at third base, which is the seat immediately to the dealer's right. Many dyed-in-the-wool blackjack players swear this is the most important player at the table. The thinking is that how this person plays his cards determines the cards that the dealer gets.

I don't agree. Half the time a poor player at third base will help the dealer, and half the time he'll do just the opposite—so in the long run it isn't really important where you sit. After all, you're playing your cards against the dealer's cards, and how anyone else plays their cards shouldn't really matter. In fact, I like the last seat. It gives me more time to think about how I want to play my hand.

Craps: Always make your bets while the dice are in the center of the table. As soon as the stickman gives the dice to the shooter, no more bets are allowed. If you take odds on your pass line bet, leave a couple of inches so the dice don't get cocked between your chips. When shooting the dice, you're free to let 'em fly as soon as the stickman gives them to you. If you're betting against the shooter, don't whoop and holler when you win. Remember, everyone else at the table probably lost.

Don't throw your chips at the dealer when making a bet. Place the chips on the table within the dealer's reach. When making a proposition bet, toss the chip flat side down to the stickman and tell him what you want. Make sure he hears you; it gets noisy in the casinos.

When you're shooting, try not to throw the dice off the table. Now you've thrown the whole game out of sync, everyone's gonna lose, and it's all your fault. If it does happen, though, tell the stickman you want the same dice. That lets the other players know you're no novice at this game, and in the eyes of the others you'll be elevated to a hero's status. Even if you lose now, it wasn't your fault. After all, you did ask for the same dice. If that doesn't work, then just swallow the dice. This will make everybody laugh, and it's hard for them to hurt you when they're laughing.

Always make your bets before the stickman gives the dice to the shooter. Once the shooter's got the dice, hands up. If the dice hit your hand at a crap game, it's an automatic five-to-fifteen-year prison sentence.

Roulette: If you can't reach a certain number, ask the dealer to place the bet for you. Other players will also help you if you ask. Remember, though, it's your responsibility to make sure the bets are on the right numbers.

The dealer will wave his hand over the table when the ball starts to slow down. No more bets are allowed from that point.

Don't lean on the plastic shield separating the players from the roulette wheel. When you win, wait until the dealer removes the marker (which he places on the winning number) before picking up your money. Convert your roulette chips into regular chips before leaving. Roulette chips are only good at the roulette wheel.

Baccarat: Be sure to settle your banker commission before leaving the table. The dealer has marked the amount you owe, and it's your obligation to pay that commission before you leave. At mini-baccarat, the dealer will usually take the commission on winning banker bets after the hand, subtracting it from your payoff. Leave the change on the table. From that point on, the dealer will take the commissions out of your change.

Pai Gow & Pai Gow Poker: Always keep your cards or tiles over the table. It's also considered proper etiquette to refrain from setting your hands until after the dealer has removed the dice bowl—which is used to determine the first hand.

Slots: If a machine is unoccupied, it's considered

good etiquette to ask the player at the next machine if he's playing that one as well, since many players like to play two machines at once. If you need to leave your machine for a moment, place an empty cup on your chair or over the machine's handle.

Race and Sports Books: Don't sit at a chair where there's a newspaper or racing form. That usually means someone else is already sitting there. Make your bets before you go to the window. Allow yourself plenty of time at the window because chances are some creep in front of you will ask the clerk, "Uh, what's a trifecta?"

2
Slot Machines

Do the odds change on the slot machines when I only play one coin?

No, but you should always play the maximum number of coins. Most machines pay a bonus on jackpots hit with the maximum coins invested, and that makes it worth the extra investment. Let me tell you what happened to one woman in 1997. She was playing a Megabucks slot machine with a jackpot of over $12 million. She started with $100, playing three coins every spin. Down to her last dollar, she plunked it in the machine and pulled the handle. Three Megabucks symbols lined up. Instead of winning $12 million, she got a secondary jackpot of $5,000—which was just about enough to pay her attorney fees when her husband filed for divorce.

What are the odds of hitting a Megabucks slot machine?

The game's innovator won't say, but mathematician John Robison has the figures. "Although each (of the three reels) has 22 physical stops," he writes in *Chance and Circumstance* magazine, "the machine is programmed to *pretend* that each reel has 368 virtual stops on each reel." So multiplying 368 X 368 X 368 makes the odds 49,836,031 to 1.

What kind of regular reel machine should I play?

Look for slot carousels with progressive jackpots. You won't get as many secondary jackpots, but the big pay-offs can be as high as a million dollars. Some even offer free cars. Now you can drive to the poor house in style.

Remember, though, that you're giving up a lot of smaller payoffs for a chance to win the big one.

Should I join a casino slot club?

Absolutely. This way you get credit every time you play the machines, and you'll be eligible for discounted room rates, free meals, and other casino goodies—plus you can use the card to scrape the ice off your car's wind-shield. Many slot clubs set aside blocks of rooms for their players during busy times of the year, and if you're a slot club member you may be able to get a room when nobody else can. Even if you don't plan to play the machines, join the slot club anyway. Sometimes you get a free gift just for signing up. At the very least, you're now on the casi-no's mailing list, which means you'll start getting coin vouchers, meal discounts, and room deals throughout the year.

Don't be tempted to rack up more slot club points by staying at a machine longer. Instead, look for special pro-motions when double or even triple points are offered. If you can afford it, play dollar slots instead of quarters dur-ing these promotions. Your points will climb four times faster!

Are all slot clubs the same?

No, they're not. Some offer cash back, others only

offer merchandise. Accumulated points at one slot club won't get you as much in merchandise as they will in another, so check out each club before you join. Here's what can happen. A friend of mine joined a slot club at an older casino on the Boulder Highway. After playing the machines for a year, he had amassed 16,000 points. What did he get for all those points?

"One free night in our R.V. park," the woman behind the club counter announced proudly.

"I don't have an R.V.," my friend replied. "Is it okay if I just spend the night there in my car?"

Check out the rules of the slot club when you sign up. Find out if there are any restrictions or limits. Make sure your slot card is inserted properly into the machine so you get credit for the time you play. And don't forget to remove your card when you're through playing.

Which casino in Las Vegas instituted the first slot club?

The first slot club in Vegas was the Golden Nugget's 24 Karat Club. It opened in 1984. The first member of the club (000-000-001) was Mrs. Henry Davenport, who has already accumulated enough points for two buffet tickets and a Golden Nugget T-shirt.

Does the machine pay more often if you use a slot card?

No, the use of a slot card doesn't affect the machine in any way.

Are the slot machines near the front door set to pay back more than the other machines in the casino?

Here's what a slot technician told us. "They can be. The chip inside each denomination of machine will have a different hold percentage. You can choose what percentage goes into what machine. So machines by the front door can be set differently, yes, but I've never heard of anyone doing it."

Can a slot machine be sent remote commands from a back room or programmed in any other way to keep me playing longer?

The casino industry is closely regulated, and state gaming laws prohibit any such subterfuge. Slot machines "must use a random selection process to determine the outcome of each play. Elements which produce winning or losing game outcomes must be available for random selection at the initiation of each play." The same gaming regulation also states that results of the random selection process "must not result in any recognizable dependency upon previous game outcome, the amount wagered, or upon the style or method of play."

How do I know when a slot machine is due to hit?

It may be due; it may be overdue. You'll never know, however, and neither will the machine. Every play is completely independent of every other play, and the random number generator inside each machine has no memory of what happened before.

In video poker machines, the random number generator is constantly running, and selects a random number from the card sequence every 1/1,000th of a second! The selection process can be programmed by the manufacturer to start at the moment the coin is inserted, the moment the coin is accepted, the moment the coin is registered, or at the exact instant the player hits the "deal" button.

(Thanks to Dwight Crevelt, author of *Video Poker Mania*, for this insight. I thought there was a midget inside the machine.)

Does a slot machine know how many coins I have inserted?

No, and it doesn't care. A reel slot machine is designed to pay back a certain percentage of the money it takes in, and due to intense competition these percentages are roughly the same wherever you play. Your chances of hitting a big jackpot, or even lining up a couple of cherries, are the same whether you put in one coin or the maximum. When you play a reel machine, all you're doing is hoping that the three reels—or four reels—or God forbid five reels—are going to line up on identical symbols and make you rich. Keep in mind that there are thousands of different combinations on these machines, and the E-Prom (Erasable Programmable Read-Only Memory) inside each machine has already decided how much of your money it will keep.

If I don't win anything on one slot machine, should I go to another one?

You can if you want, but it doesn't really matter. The machines are set to pay back a certain percentage and keep the rest, but the rule to remember is that it's all long-term. At video poker, the averages say you'll get a royal flush once every 40,000 hands. So technically, it's all the same whether you play 40,000 hands on one machine, or 10 hands on 4,000 different machines, or 100 hands on 400 machines.

Personally, I change machines sometimes, but it's not because the machine is cold. It's because the woman sitting next to me is smoking a cigar.

I've heard that you have a better chance of winning if you play the machine as fast as you can. Is there anything to this?

No, the speed at which you play doesn't change anything. The random number generator inside the machine is the only determining factor as to whether you're going to win or not. You're better off taking your time. At least, your money will last longer.

On progressive slot machines, how much does the progressive meter rise for each coin played?

The rate is based on a pre-set percentage of all the money cycled through the machine, and varies from machine to machine, and casino to casino. According to casino expert Mark Pilarski, you can usually expect the meter to climb anywhere from 5 to 10% of the coins played on an individual progressive. Example: Play a dollar, and the jackpot goes up 10¢. On carousels or super jackpot progressives, like Quarter Mania or Megabucks, the jackpot won't climb as rapidly. Then again, what's the difference whether you win $14,356,000 or $14,356,000 and 10¢?

Are there any strategies I should use when I play a slot machine?

Always play the maximum number of coins. Most slot machines pay a bonus on jackpots hit with the maximum number of coins played.

Cash out your credits frequently, and set time limits when you play.

Set cash limits, and stick to them.

Keep records of losses as well as winnings.

I like to play the slots when I'm depressed. It seems to make all my problems disappear for a while.

Bad idea. Slot machines are programmed to be at their best, 24 hours a day. You should be at your best, too. If you've got other things on your mind, or if you're tired or sleepy, the machines have got you at a big disadvantage. Tackle the slots while you're refreshed and clear-headed, and you'll give yourself a better chance of winning.

> **TIP: Treat yourself to a software computer program such as** *Stanford Wong Video Poker* **or** *Bob Dancer's Win Poker.* **I've got 'em both. You play the hands and the computer beeps you if you make a mistake. You'll be surprised how quickly you can learn the optimum strategy at this—beep—tantalizing—beep—game.**

What are the most common mistakes people make when playing video poker?

Drawing to an inside straight (except on deuces wild or joker machines), keeping a kicker (high card) with a pair, and holding three cards of the same suit to make a flush. The odds are against you making any of these hands, and they don't pay that much anyway. Another suggestion: Concentrate on one type of machine, such as deuces wild. Learn the basic strategy for that game, and then stick to it. It's hard to become an expert on every kind of machine in the casino, but not that difficult to become an expert on one.

Why is it so hard to find a nickel slot machine?

You just have to know where to look. Lower denomination machines are usually found near the self-parking garages and snack bars. The thinking is that if you can't afford to valet park your car or eat a decent meal, then you're also going to gamble for nickels and dimes. On the other hand, higher denomination machines will be found near the gourmet restaurants, the nice shops, and other expensive attractions.

What's the quickest way to find a slot machine in my price range?

Most of the newer slot machines have colored lights on top that signify the machine's denomination. A red light means it's a 5¢ machine; green means 10¢; yellow means 25¢, orange means 50¢, blue means $1, and purple signifies $5. If you see a flashing light on the machine, it usually means the coin hopper on that machine is almost empty. Hopefully, the attendant will see it, too, and refill the machine.

Who invented the slot machine?

The original Liberty Bell slot machine (named in honor of the nation's symbol of freedom) was invented in 1895 by Charles Fey of San Francisco. Only three of Fey's machines are still around, and each is worth upwards of $100,000.

How did the fruit and bell symbols on slot machines originate?

Before gambling was legalized, slot machines would dispense a stick of gum with each pull of the handle. You were gambling, but you were getting something back for your money, so you—er—weren't really gambling. Bell was a popular brand of gum at the time, and the gum came in orange, cherry, plum, and lemon.

What are the odds of hitting a royal flush on a video poker machine?

Better sit down for this one. The odds of hitting a royal are about 40,000 to 1, or about once every 70 hours of play. On the other hand, the odds of being dealt a royal on your first 5 cards are 649,739-1.

What are the odds of hitting a sequential royal?

The attraction of hitting a royal in sequence (A-K-Q-J-10) is winning a jackpot that can be as high as $100,000 in some casinos. The odds of hitting a sequential royal, however, are about 4.7 million to 1. To figure it another way, if you played 40 hours a week, you'd hit one of these babies once every two years!

What are the odds of turning a pair into three-of-a-kind?

Twenty-two to 1. Here are some other interesting statistics. The odds of turning two pair into a full house are 11-1. The odds of drawing one card to make an inside straight are 11-1. The odds of making a straight out of a four-card open straight are 5-1. The odds of making a flush out of a four-card flush are 4-1.

How are the cards dealt in video poker machines?

A regular 52-card deck is used, and the cards are reshuffled after each hand. The random number generator—which changes every fraction of a second—locks five cards into place the instant you press the "deal" button. If you draw two cards, you either get the next two off the deck, or the cards will continue to be shuffled until you press the "draw" button. Either way, the probability of drawing to a winning hand remain the same, so don't worry about it. It's all random, and so are your chances of winning.

What kind of video poker machine should I look for?

The first thing you should do when you sit down at any video poker machine is look at the payoffs for the full house and flush on the award glass. The payout for a full house should be 9 coins per coin played; the payout for a flush should be 6 coins per coin played. This is known as a "9-6 machine." Do not play a machine that pays 8 coins for a full house and 5 for a flush. Technically, you're throwing away your original investment every time you get a full house or flush.

What are those horse-racing machines I've seen in some casinos?

The Sigma Horse Derby is kind of like a fancy slot machine, with little metal horses instead of little metal reels. There are five horses in each race, but you can only make quinella wagers (in other words, a bet on any two horses who must finish first and second in either order). Before the race starts, the odds are posted on all quinella bets.

In the race I watched, the 3-4 combination was a 2-1 favorite, and the 2-5 combination was a 200-1 longshot. Not surprisingly, the favorite won. According to a Sigma spokesperson, the most popular strategy employed by players is to "load up on the favorites, then drop a coin or two on the long shot for a possible big win."

Does the slot attendant know which machines are hot or cold?

Sure, she's been watching them all day. She can tell you which machines have been hit in the last few hours, and which ones have been played without success. She has no way of knowing when a machine is due to hit, though. She's just giving you a tip, and if you hit the machine she's going to expect a tip, too.

What if I have 500 credits and need to leave my machine?

Tell a slot attendant to watch your machine until you return, then place an empty change cup on your seat to let others know your machine is occupied. If you don't see an attendant, then ask the player at the next machine to watch yours for you until you return. If the player at the next machine needs a shave and is wearing track shoes, cash out your credits and take your money with you.

Should I play in a slot tournament?

Casino tournaments can be a lot of fun, but remember you're bucking the casino odds and the other tournament participants. Advantages of playing in a tournament: Room, meals, and special parties are usually included in the price. Disadvantage: The price! It can be as high as $10,000, and only the top winners end up in the money. That's the main reason why only 3% of the people who come to Las Vegas play in gaming tournaments.

Do I have to pay taxes on my winnings?

You must pay taxes on any slot machine jackpot of over $1,200, and winnings of over $1,500 at bingo and keno. You'll get a W-2G form (the "G" stands for gambling) at the time you're paid. So keep track of your losses by holding onto your coin wrappers, because these can be subtracted from your winnings. Or join a slot club. Then at the end of the year, ask for a "Win/Loss Statement for Slot Play" and now you've got it all in writing. For more information, contact my accountant: Mr. Hugo Diddlemeyer, Cell 239, Nevada State Penitentiary, Carson City, Nevada.

There are no taxes on table game winnings—yet! The I.R.S. has no way of knowing how much you lost at the tables. When you win a bundle at blackjack, you keep it all!

Do people from other countries have to pay taxes on their winnings?

Good question. I called the Internal Revenue Service and got the following recorded message. "If you're being audited, press One. If you're requesting a tax extension, press Two. If you're calling in a bomb threat, press Three. If you're from another country and want to know if you have to pay taxes on your gambling winnings, press Four." I pressed Four, and got the following information.

"The United States has income tax treaties with a number of foreign countries. Under these treaties, residents of foreign countries are taxed at a reduced rate, or are exempt from U.S. income taxes on certain items of income they receive from sources within the United States. These reduced rates and exemptions vary among countries and specific items of income."

The casino industry puts it a little more clearly. Read the memorandum on the next page, which was distributed to all Nevada casinos in 1995. Since that date, some countries may have been added and others may not even be countries now. Your best bet is to contact the I.R.S. for detailed information before you leave the United States. If you are taxed on gambling winnings, the same scale applies: any slot machine jackpot of over $1,200, and winnings of over $1,500 at bingo and keno.

When will the slot machine pay me, and when will I be paid by a slot attendant?

The machine will usually pay you on all non-taxable jackpots. Sometimes, though, the machine may run out of coins before you're completely paid. In that case, a message will appear on the screen saying "Call Attendant." You won't even have to leave your seat because there's a button on the machine that will bring the attendant. In no case should you play the machine again until the attendant comes, because she has no way of verifying your win.

MEMORANDUM

DATE: December 15, 1995
TO:
FROM:
RE: TAX EXEMPT COUNTRIES–1042S FORMS

Please be advised that effective immediately, the following countries have come to an agreement with the United States that a tax withholding rate of 30% is **not required**.

1.	Czech Republic	9.	Portugal
2.	Finland	10.	Russian Federation
3.	France	11.	Slovak Republic
4.	Germany	12.	Spain
5.	Hungary	13.	Sweden
6.	Italy	14.	Tunisia
7.	Malta	15.	Ukraine
8.	Netherlands	16.	United Kingdom

In order for a patron to qualify they must produce a passport from their respective country.

If you have any questions, please feel free to contact me at ext. 7050. Thank you

CC:

If I win a big jackpot, will the casino take my picture?

Only if you let 'em. From the casino's standpoint, it looks good that someone actually won something on one of their machines. From your standpoint, it's not such a good idea. Let me put it this way. Do you want your name and hometown splashed in the newspaper, along with the fact that you just won a million dollars in Vegas? You'll be a celebrity for about three days, and a recluse for the rest of your life—spending all your winnings on home security, bodyguards, karate lessons, rocket launchers, bullet-proof vests, and a private answering service to screen telephone calls from needy friends, relatives, and gaming book authors.

When will I get paid?

Right away, unless it's a giant jackpot like Megabucks—and then you'll get your money in annual installments or in a lump sum payment. Of course, the first thing the casino will do is open the machine to make sure you won the money legitimately. To get technical about it, there's a sealed microprocessor with a serial number inside the machine. There's also a lead seal with a wire that goes through the microprocessor, and this seal has a casino stamp on it. After these are checked, a casino technician will use a device called a "chipsum" to verify that the microprocessor hasn't been switched. Don't be insulted. There are a lot of slot cheats roaming the streets and the casino is just being careful. While you're waiting, have a free drink, and think about which charities you want to give all that money to.

When you hit a hit a big jackpot like Megabucks, the machine will lock up so that you don't accidentally erase the winning symbols. This can result in some amazing stories. An Asian man inserted a $10 bill into a Megabucks machine and on his first spin won the progressive jackpot of $21 million. When told how much money he'd won, his first question was, "Where my other seven dollar?"

One sleepy morning I was walking through Caesars Palace when a woman stopped me to complain that her machine wouldn't work. I looked at the symbols on her machine, then told her, "Ma'am, you just won a new car!"

Speaking of cars, here's a true story that happened some 20 years ago in a Vegas casino. A woman lined up three winning symbols for a new Buick. After all the paperwork had been filled out, she was asked to play off the winning symbols to re-set the machine. She put in three more quarters—and won another Buick!

Where can I find a penny slot machine?

Penny slot machines are almost impossible to find any-more, although the Gold Spike in downtown Las Vegas has a whole bank of penny video poker machines. The most you can hope to win on one, though, is a whopping $7.50—which is what it's going to cost you in cab fare to get to the Gold Spike.

Where should I play?

If you're trying to rack up points on your slot card, or get credit for the time you play at a table game, you should concentrate on one casino—preferably where you're staying. If you want the most for your money, play in downtown Las Vegas or at one of the city's neighbor-hood casinos. Slots are usually looser, proposition payoffs on the table games are higher, and food is cheaper. It's also crowded and noisy, and most of the patrons are wear-ing hard hats. That's why I prefer relaxing in my pent-house apartment overlooking the Strip, and having my valet make my bets for me.

Where's the worst place to play a slot machine?

I would never play a slot machine in a bar. These

machines are usually screwed down so tight that you couldn't get any money out of one with a jackhammer. A point to remember, though, is that in Nevada no slot machine can hold over 25%. So figure that most slot bars will keep the max. You're already inside drinking, so they're not too worried about you staggering somewhere else.

If a slot machine advertises 90% payback, does that mean I should wind up with $90 if I invest $100?

Technically, yes. The problem, though, is that most players will re-invest that $90, and now you're down to $81 (multiply $90 by 90%). If you try a third time, again on the average, there's around $73 left. After seven cycles, that $100 has shrunk to $49, or more than half of what you started with. So although the payback percentage is accurate, it can be misleading.

Can I have a slot machine in my home?

Most states allow a person to own a slot machine if it is not being used for gambling. Slot machine expert Dan Mead wrote, "Since 1990, more favorable laws have allowed casino-type machines to be purchased by the general public. The trend now seems to be 'game room machines,' and not collectibles per se. We are finding more and more that people want slot machines to play; not to look at." Laws vary, though, from state to state. In Massachusetts, for example, mechanical slot machines are legal if they're 30 years old, but poker machines are legal for personal home use. It wouldn't hurt to check with the Attorney General's office in your state before buying a slot machine.

If you decide to buy one, Mead's Loose Change Blue Book lists the prices and grades on all reconditioned machines (702-387-8750 for more info). Gambler's

General Store in Las Vegas has a full line of casino sup-
plies, including slot machines, poker chips, layouts, cards,
dice—and all my books (702-382-9903).

3
Blackjack

When I play blackjack, I'm always afraid the dealer will go too fast.

The casino would like to deal 60 hands an hour at each blackjack table. But if you're not sure whether you want another card or not, what's the dealer going to do? He's going to wait for you to make a decision. Take your time, and play at your own pace. The dealer will wait, and so will every other player at the table.

What happens if my hand ties the dealer's hand?

On a total of 17 or more, it's called a "push," and no money changes hands. On a total of 16 or less, remember that the dealer has to take another card. Every day I hear someone say, "But I've only got 13, and if the dealer has 14 I've already lost." NO! The dealer must hit any hand under 17.

If the dealer has the advantage at blackjack, shouldn't I play the same way that he does?

No. The reason the dealer has the advantage is because you've got to make your decision before he makes his. If you bust, and then the dealer busts, he's already won your money. The dealer doesn't get paid extra for a blackjack. He can't split pairs, and he can't double down. You can, and by knowing when to split and when to double down, you can get the house edge down to under 1%.

When I split pairs, do I get as many cards as I want on each hand?

Yes, except when you split aces. You only get one card on each ace, and the dealer will place that card sideways—which means that's all the cards you'll get.

When should I split 10s?

Here's the way one veteran blackjack dealer explained it. "The only time you split 10s is when you're drunk."

I've heard that you're supposed to split 9s on certain occasions. I already have a good hand, don't I?

Yes, you do. But if the dealer is showing a 2, 3, 4, 5, or 6 you've got the odds in your favor that you're going to beat him by splitting 9s—and you're getting more money in the game. By the same token, you should also split 9s if the dealer is showing an 8 or 9. That way, you're giving yourself a better chance of beating or tying the dealer.

Should I hit a 12 if the dealer is showing a 2?

Yes. The dealer has a 42% chance of making a better hand out of a 12. That means you have the same chance to better your hand. For the same reason, you should also hit a 12 if the dealer is showing a 3. In the long run, you'll be money ahead.

Why are the cards dealt face up in most casinos?

Most casinos deal the cards face up to keep the players from bending, crimping, or marking the cards. Many novice players don't like the idea that everyone else can see their cards, but dealing the cards face up doesn't change anything—and the game usually goes faster.

Why is the game called blackjack?

When the game was first introduced, you were paid extra money if one of your first two cards was a black jack. Now it's any 10-count card and an ace. Casino insiders, however, refer to the game as "21."

How often can I expect to get a blackjack?

Statistically, you should get a blackjack once every 21 hands.

How often will the dealer bust?

Not very often. According to statistics, the dealer will bust on fewer than three out of every 10 hands—except at the game where you're playing. Then he never busts.

How often will the dealer make a good hand if he is showing a 5 or 6?

Roughly 58% of the time. So the optimum strategy here is to stand with a bad hand, since the dealer should bust almost half the time.

How often will the dealer bust if he is showing an ace?

Mathematically, there's only an 11.5% probability of the dealer busting when he's showing an ace. Therefore, you've got to hit a bad hand against an ace, since nine out of ten times the dealer will beat you if you don't.

I got a blackjack and the dealer turned over an ace. Before offering the other players insurance,

he asked if I wanted even money for my black-jack. What did that mean?

He was offering to pay you without knowing before-hand if he had a blackjack, too. Actually, taking even money for a blackjack is the same thing as taking insur-ance. Example: You have a $10 bet, and the dealer offers you insurance. You place $5 in the insurance box. The dealer turns over a blackjack. Your $10 bet is a push, and you get paid 2 to 1 for your $5 insurance bet. You win $10, or even money.

In my opinion, taking even money isn't a bad idea. You're going to win something whether the dealer has a blackjack or not.

It seems that every time I get a good run of cards at blackjack, the casino switches dealers. Why do they do that?

Blackjack dealers get a break every hour—and after an hour of dealing to boozers and losers, they need one. That's the only reason any reputable casino changes deal-ers.

Odds of the dealer busting in a multi-deck game if his up-card is:	
2	35.4%
3	37.4%
4	39.4%
5	41.6%
6	42.3%
7	26.2%
8	24.5%
9	22.8%
10	21.2%
Ace	11.5%

What do you call a basement full of blackjack players?

A whine cellar?

Why does the dealer alert the supervisor before shuffling the cards?

It's a precautionary measure taken by the casino to ensure that the cards are shuffled properly. The supervisor will also watch when a player cuts the cards, and while the cards are inserted back into the shoe.

Sometimes when I cut the cards, the dealer will ask me to cut them again. Is there a reason for this, or is the dealer just being picky?

The old expression "cut thin and win" doesn't work in the casino. If you're playing single-deck blackjack, you must cut at least ten cards into the deck. At multiple-deck shoes, the house rule is that you must cut the cards at least one deck into the rest.

Incidentally, be careful with the cut card the dealer offers you. It not only cuts the cards; it can also cut the dealer's finger.

What happens if nobody wants to cut the cards at the blackjack table?

In that case, the dealer will cut them. If the dealer doesn't, then the floor supervisor will. If he doesn't, then the pit boss will. If he doesn't, then the shift boss will. If he doesn't, then the casino manager will. If he doesn't, then the vice president in charge of casino operations will. If he doesn't, the cards will be flown to the owner's villa in Paris, and he'll cut them when he gets good and ready. In the meantime, just think of all the free drinks you're getting.

BASIC STRATEGY

Player Has:	Dealer is Showing
10	Double down 3 through 6
11	Double down except Ace
12	Stand 4 through 6
13-16	Stand 2 through 6
17-21	Stand
A2-A3	Double down 5 or 6
A4-A5	Double down 4 through 6
A6	Double down 3 through 6, otherwise hit
A7	Double down 3 through 6; Hit on 9, 10, A
A8-A10	Always stand
A,A	Always split
2,2	Split 2 through 7
3,3	Split 2 through 7
4,4	Split 5 or 6 (Optional)
5,5	Double down 2 through 9
6,6	Split 2 through 6
7,7	Split 2 through 7
8,8	Always split
9,9	Split unless 7, 10, or A
10, 10	Always stand

What is that small viewfinder I see on some blackjack tables?

It's a relatively new innovation called a scanner. The dealer looks into it to see if he has a blackjack, and the scanner (some use flashing lights) lets the dealer know whether his bottom card is a 10 or ace.

When the dealer places the cards in the shoe, why does he take the first card and place it in the discard rack?

That's called "burning" a card, and when you get right down to it most players would probably prefer that the dealer burned all the cards. The reason is to discourage card counters, since nobody knows the value of that card.

If I'm having an exceptionally bad run of cards, can I ask the dealer to stop the game and re-shuffle?

Sure. The dealer will have to get an okay from his supervisor, but in most instances the dealer will be allowed to re-shuffle.

What is the proper etiquette for leaving the table?

If you're coming right back, ask the dealer to save your seat. He'll usually place a clear plastic box over your chips until your return. If you're not planning to return, just get up and go. Here's the way one blackjack dealer explained it to a novice player: "Hey, there ain't any seat belts on those chairs, honey."

When should I quit?

That's hard to answer because when you're winning you want to win more, and when you lose you want to win back what you lost. My suggestion is to set a limit each

time you gamble. If you double it, walk away. If you lose
it, limp away.

If the dealer is on a hot streak, should I go to another table?

I usually stay where I am, especially if I'm with a fun
group of players. After all, winning streaks and losing
streaks occur randomly in any game of chance. When the
dealer cools off, your level of skill will pay off, and you'll be
back in the chips again. Don't let frustration get the best
of you. Play your game, and wait for the cards to turn.

What is "Surrender"?

It's an option offered in most casinos, whereby you're
allowed to surrender half your bet if you don't like your
first two cards (and if the dealer does not have a blackjack). Most experts say you should surrender if you've got
a 15 and the dealer is showing a 10, or if you've got 16
(except two 8s) and the dealer is showing a 9, 10, or ace.
Personally, I would never surrender. The dealer may turn
over a bad card and wind up busting, and here you've
already given up half your original bet. Give yourself a
chance. Stay in the game.

Of course, there are exceptions to every rule. A well-
heeled gambler, with a credit line of $62,500, ran into a
streak of bad luck at the blackjack table. Down to his last
$500 bet, he was dealt a 17. The dealer was showing a
10, so the player surrendered half his bet. Sure enough,
the dealer had a 20, and now the man was down to $250.
He bet it all, won the next hand, parlayed the $500 to
$1,000, then $2,000. Twenty minutes later, the man had
won back his $62,500, plus another $30,000—all because
he surrendered half of his last $500 bet.

Are the odds more in my favor at a single deck blackjack game, or against a shoe?

There's the same ratio of big cards and small cards, whether the dealer is using one deck or half a dozen. It's easier to keep track of the cards at single deck blackjack, but single deck games are almost impossible to find.

I like shoes because more options are generally available. You can usually split pairs up to four times, double down on any two cards, double after splitting, surrender, and play for higher stakes. Many of these options are generally not available at single-deck games.

Another reason why shoes are more popular is because the dealer can deal four to five times as many hands without stopping to re-shuffle the cards. After all, when the cards are being shuffled, no money is changing hands.

Does card counting really work at blackjack?

"With perfect card counting and perfect rules, such as a single deck dealt down to the last card and the unlimited right to vary the size of bets, it becomes a statistical certainty that the player will win in the long run." So writes I. Nelson Rose in his book *Gambling and the Law*. I disagree. The whole theory behind card counting is that you're taking the advantage away from the casino when you know the deck is rich in large cards. But doesn't the dealer have the same opportunity? Besides, no casino deals the deck right down to the last card. In fact, you're lucky to even find a single-deck or double-deck game.

The advantage of counting cards is that you can vary your bets according to your count, and there's nothing wrong with that. Another advantage of a deck rich in large cards is that if you get a blackjack, you get paid three to two. (The dealer only gets back even money.) For those who want to try it, here's how card counting works: Use a plus count for each small card (2 through 6) that's dealt, and a minus count for 10s and aces. Whenever the count becomes plus 4 or more, the deck is supposedly ripe for the counter. According to some experts, an increase of just one unit is enough to give a good counter a favorable opportunity.

You can try card counting if you want. But if you suddenly increase your bet from $5 to $500, just because there are a lot of 10s in the deck, the dealer is usually going to stop the game and re-shuffle the cards. Then you're right back where you started.

Here's another problem facing the card counter. He might have $25,000 in his arsenal, whereas the casino has millions of dollars in its arsenal. For the solitary card counter, it's like an ant going up against an anteater. Consequently, the latest scheme by card counting experts is to employ an *army* of ants. One counter is in charge of the betting strategy, another counts the cards, a third studies the dealer's shuffle, breaking the shoe down into segments that are either rich in small cards or rich in big cards.

This blackjack wolf pack will usually hit a table during a busy holiday weekend, when the floor supervisor is busy with paperwork. By the time he realizes he's got real pros on the game, it's too late. Some of these card counting teams have actually set themselves up as legitimate corporations, selling shares at $1,000 apiece to hundreds of individuals around the country. Now they've got a sizable arsenal to pit against the casino's.

So yes, in that respect, card counting can work, and the casinos are already at work on ways to combat it.

Should I ever play hunches?

Absolutely not. That is, unless you—er—have a really good hunch.

If I get five cards without going over 21, do I automatically win?

No, even though it's a great idea. However, you win

automatically at the Las Vegas Club in downtown Las Vegas if you get six cards without going over 21.

In some casinos the dealer hits a soft 17, and in some casinos the dealer stands on a soft 17. Why aren't the rules the same in every casino?

Each casino has its own list of options—and unfortunately these options are not always to the player's advantage. For example, hitting a soft 17 (ace and a 6) adds an additional .02% to the casino's edge. That's why you should check before you play. It'll tell you right on the blackjack table whether the dealer hits a soft 17 or not. Look for a table where the dealer must stand on all 17s.

What is the most common mistake that blackjack players make?

Standing on a soft 17. Seventeen is a borderline hand. It isn't a bad hand and it isn't a good hand. By hitting a soft 17, the following cards will give you a better hand: ace, 2, 3, and 4—and a 10 still gives you a 17. So out of 13 different card combinations, only 5 cards can hurt you. Besides, the dealer will keep drawing until he gets to 17, and then the best you can do is tie him.

What else can I do to give myself a better chance of winning?

For one thing, don't make the same bet every single hand. Think about it. If the casino has the advantage to begin with, and you make the same bet every hand, what's going to happen to you? If you expect to win, you must use money management: increasing your bet when you win and decreasing your bet when you lose.

Another overlooked strategy at blackjack is what to do with "soft" hands—such as ace-2, ace-3, ace-4. For example, how many cards will give you a better hand with an ace and 4? Six out of 13, and a 10 won't hurt you.

If the dealer is showing a 5 or 6, you should double down with A-2, A-3, A-4, A-5, A-6, and even A-7. You've got the odds in your favor, so you want to get as much money in the game as you can.

Do I have to specify what an ace is worth at the beginning of the hand?

No, you can change the value of an ace at any time. An ace can be confusing to some novice players, so here's an easy way to determine an ace's value. If an ace won't help your hand, count it as 1. If it will help your hand, count it as 11. If that doesn't help, count the ace as a 1 and then add 10 to it. Example: ace and 6 is 7, plus 10 equals 17.

Other strategies with an ace:

- Always hit an ace-6 (a soft 17). You've got a free card coming, four of which will give you a better hand—and if you get a 10, you still have 17.
- Never hit an ace-8 or an ace-9. You already have a great hand.
- Hit an ace-7 if the dealer is showing a 9, 10, or ace.

How do I know what the minimum bet is on a blackjack table?

There's a sign on each table in the casino that tells you what the minimum (and maximum) bet is. You can also tell by the color of the sign, which matches the color of the chips: red for $5, green for $25, and black for $100.

I like to play blackjack, but I can't find a low-stake table. Why don't the casinos have any $2 tables?

It's almost impossible to bet less than $5 on the Strip,

but you can still find $2 tables in downtown Las Vegas and in some neighborhood casinos. If you want to stay on the Strip, play during off times (Monday through Thursday, early morning or early afternoon). If it's quiet, the casino might lower the stakes. Here's another tip. Take a learner's class at the casino. Afterwards, the casino usually sets up a $2 table for its students, and you can play as long as you want.

What if I'm playing at a $5 table and the dealer suddenly raises the minimum bet to $25?

You'll usually be "grandfathered in," which means you can keep betting $5 while all the new players have to bet $25.

Can I bet on somebody else's hand?

You can, but why would you want to? This practice is called "piggy back" betting, and it's popular in Europe where there are more blackjack players than there are tables. In Las Vegas, there are plenty of tables to go around, so the idea of betting on somebody else's hand isn't that popular. If you want to do it, though, go ahead—but get the player's permission first.

How many decks are in a shoe?

At blackjack, most casinos use six decks of cards.

Why is the card-holder called a shoe?

Because it's shaped like a shoe! The shoe, or sabot as it's called in French, is an oblong box with the front end covered by a rubber faceplate. Through a slit in the bottom of this faceplate, the dealer slides out the cards. You'll notice that the shoe is also chained to the table, making it almost impossible for somebody to replace the shoe with another one.

Can I use basic strategy on a video blackjack machine?

Yes. Cards are dealt from a regular 52-card deck at video blackjack, and you can use the same strategy that you use at the blackjack tables. Although playing against a machine is not as much fun, you can play for as little as 25¢ a hand. Most of the new machines also pay you automatically if you're dealt six cards without busting.

The disadvantages of playing video blackjack far outweigh the advantages.The maximum bet is usually 20 coins, and the cards are shuffled after each hand. The biggest drawback, however, is that you're only paid even money for a blackjack rather than 3-2. This bumps the house edge up another 2.5%!

I've seen basic strategy cards on sale in the casino gift shops. Can I use these cards at the blackjack tables?

Most casinos don't care if you use a basic strategy card while you play. There are exceptions, though, so check before sitting down at the table.

Should I look for a crowded table, or should I play by myself?

Some people will only play heads-up against the dealer, again with the thinking that nobody else can screw up their cards. Remember, though, if you're the only player at the table, the game goes much faster, and so does your bankroll. I like to play on a crowded game. It's usually a lot more fun.

Can I play two hands or more at a blackjack game?

Yes, but some casinos will make you bet double the minimum on each hand you play. Personally, I prefer to play only one hand at a time. Otherwise, you might get one good hand and one bad one, and wind up not winning anything.

What is "Double Exposure" blackjack?

It's a game dealt by a topless dealer. No! "Double Exposure" blackjack is a variation of regular blackjack, only in this game both of the dealer's cards are dealt face up. It sounds great, but avoid this one at all costs. The dealer wins pushes; surrender and resplits are not allowed; you can only double down on certain cards; and a blackjack only pays even money instead of 3-2.

If I get a blackjack, do I have to give the dealer a hand signal?

Technically, yes. Read the following true story, and you'll understand why. Five people were playing blackjack at a $500 table in a fancy Vegas casino. A man walked up to the table and placed $500 in cash inside the one empty betting circle. The dealer dealt the new player a blackjack. The next player was dealt a 9 and a 2. The dealer was showing a 4, so this player doubled down. The dealer dealt this player a 10, giving him a total of 21.

"Wait a minute," the player with the blackjack cried. "I wanted to double down."

"Sir, you had a blackjack," the dealer replied politely. "I already paid you."

"But I didn't make a hand signal," the player hollered. "I was going to double down, and that 10 you just gave the other player would have been mine."

"Sir, nobody doubles down with a blackjack."

"Don't tell me how to play my cards," the player roared. "That's my 10 and I'm doubling down!"

The dealer called her supervisor, bringing the game to a halt. The supervisor finally allowed the man to double down and take the other player's 10, but not before reprimanding the dealer for not getting a hand signal. Fortunately, the player who doubled down also got a 10.

But wait, this story isn't over yet. The dealer turned over a 7, giving her a total of 11. Then she drew a 10 for a total of 21!

Instead of winning $750, the player with the blackjack wound up with a push—and didn't win anything.

The man grabbed his money and stormed away from the table. Meanwhile, all the other players broke into cheers. Sometimes it's worth $500 just to see justice done.

How do I let the dealer know when I want to split pairs or double down?

By placing more money in your betting circle, the dealer knows you're either splitting or doubling down. The only time he'll ask you is if you're dealt two 5s, since you can either split 5s or double down with 10. Tell the dealer you're doubling down. No one in their right mind would split 5s.

What is Spanish 21?

Uh, vente uno. No, seriously, Spanish 21 is a variation of regular 21 or blackjack. It's played with 48-card decks (all the ten-spot cards have been removed), which gives the house an edge of around 8% but more options on your part.

You can double down on any number of cards. If you're not happy with your double down hand, you can take back your second bet and forfeit the original wager. A player's 21 or blackjack beats the dealer's 21 or blackjack. There are bonus payoffs on special hands, including a super bonus of $1,000 to $5,000 (depending on your bet) to any player who gets three suited 7s when the dealer's top card is also a 7.

Remember, though, that since there are no ten-count cards in the deck, your strategy will be different from regular blackjack.

- Always hit a hard 12 or 13, no matter what the dealer's up card is.
- Don't split 8s against the dealer's ace.
- Don't double down with 10 against the dealer's 8, 9, 10, or ace.
- Don't double down with 11 against the dealer's 9, 10, or ace.
- Don't take insurance.

What are the blackjack dealer's pet peeves?

I posed this question to 50 dealers at the Nevada State Penitentiary, and these are the ones we could print: blaming the dealer for your rotten luck; asking her what time she gets off work; blowing smoke in her face; counting your cards out loud; and motioning for another card with your middle finger. Well, you figure it out.

The only player at the table, a man was playing blackjack for $100 a hand. A woman sat down beside him with six $25 chips. The first thing she did was exchange four of the $25 chips for a $100 chip. She lost her two remaining $25 chips, then exchanged her $100 chip for four more $25 chips. After winning two hands, she again exchanged four of the $25 chips for a $100 chip. This continued for almost half an hour before the woman finally left.

The dealer turned to the man at the table. "Boy, that woman was a real pain in the ass," he grumbled.

"Tell me about it," the man sighed. "I've been married to her for 15 years."

What does it mean when a blackjack player scratches on the table?

That means he's asking for another card. If he scratches under the table . . . well, that's another story.

4
Craps

Why do people stand at the dice tables?

No one really knows. Maybe it's so they can get to their wallets faster, or perhaps so they can reach the multitude of bets on the table. Here are my own personal thoughts on the matter. Before gambling was legalized, craps was the most popular game in illegal casinos. If a place got raided, people could run faster if they were already on their feet. When gambling was introduced in Nevada legally, the custom was already established—and it's been that way ever since.

> Want to win money at craps? Listen for noise. If you hear people hollering at a dice table, that means they're having fun. And if they're having fun . . . they're winning money!

If the odds are that the shooter at a dice table is not going to make his point, wouldn't I be better off betting against the shooter?

No, and here's why. Don't pass bets lose if the shooter rolls a 7 or 11 on the first roll. Don't pass bets win if the shooter rolls a 2 or 3 on the first roll. There are six ways to roll a 7, and two ways to roll 11—so you have eight ways of losing your don't pass bet on the first roll, and only three wins of winning.

Then, once the shooter gets a point number, you don't get to take odds like the pass line bettors. You have to lay the odds, or bet more to win less since you now have the odds in your favor. It still sounds good on paper, but if you win two bets on the don't pass and then lose one, you're almost back where you started.

For these reasons, the don't pass isn't very popular.

A novice at the dice table placed a chip on the pass line. The dice rolled past her bet, and she turned to walk away. "Where are you going?" the dealer asked her. "The point's four."

"Oh, I thought I was betting the dice wouldn't go past my chip!"

What's to keep me from betting $100 on the pass line, and having a friend of mine bet $100 on the don't pass? We won't lose anything, and now we'll be eligible for casino comps.

It sounds good, but in the long run it just won't work—and there are 12 reasons why. Actually, it's the number 12. Twelve loses on the pass line on the come out roll, and 12 is a standoff on the don't pass. That means every time a 12 rolls on the come out roll, you'll lose your $100, and your friend gets a push. Forget it. It's cheaper to buy your own meals.

What's the difference between a come bet and a place bet?

A come bet is really nothing more than a new pass line bet, only you make a come bet after the shooter already has a point. The come bet merely "comes" to the next number that rolls. You take odds on a come bet the same way you take odds on a pass line bet, and they pay the same. Advantage: You get paid the true amount for the odds, just like you do on the pass line. Disadvantages: Your original come bet has to stay on a number until the number rolls, and the number has to roll twice—once to get on the number, and then again to get off the number.

A place bet is a bet on a particular number, and you get paid for that bet every time the number rolls. Advantage: You pick the number you want, and you can take your bet down anytime you wish. Disadvantage: You don't get paid the true odds. Example: True odds on the 4 and 10 are 2 to 1 (six ways to roll a 7, three ways to roll a 4 or 10). A place bet on the 4 or 10 pays 9 to 5, a difference of $1 on each $5 bet you make. It may not sound like much, but it comes to 20%!

Here's another reason why come bets are more popular than place bets. Let's say you decide to place all four inside numbers at $10 apiece. Taking into consideration the fact you have to bet $6 to win $7 on the 6 and 8, you've invested a total of $44, and you've got to catch three numbers to show a profit. Then a loser 7 rolls, and you make the same bet on the next shooter. Now you're in trouble, because you have to catch seven numbers in order to win a measly $10.

If you do decide to make place bets, stick to the 6 and 8. The house edge on these is only 1.52%. Less attractive are the 5 and 9, where the house edge jumps to 4%. The least popular are the 4 and 10, with a house edge of 6.73%.

Do I have to bet on the pass line in order to make a come bet?

No, and that's the beauty of it. With a come bet, you can enter the game after a hand has already started. You don't have to worry whether the shooter makes his number or not. You just want him to make your number.

Remembering the Odds at Craps
A Simple Key

There are 3 ways to roll a 4 or 10
There are 4 ways to roll a 5 or 9
There are 5 ways to roll a 6 or 8
There are 6 ways to roll a 7
So the odds on the 4 and 10 are 6 to 3
or 2 to 1
The odds on the 5 and 9 are 6 to 4
or 3 to 2
And the odds on the 6 and 8 are 6 to 5

What is a don't come bet?

It's just the opposite of the come bet, only now your money comes behind the next number that rolls. So if you're on the don't come, and a 4 rolls, your money goes behind the 4—and now you're betting a 7 comes before another 4.

What does "off and on" mean?

Let's say you make a come bet and it goes to the 6. Then you make another come bet, and the shooter rolls another 6. Instead of moving your come bet off the 6, and moving your new come bet back on the 6, the dealer will simply pay you and leave your original bet on the 6. In other words, one bet goes "off" and one bet goes "on." It just saves time.

What is the field?

The field is a one-roll bet that pays you even money if 3, 4, 9, 10, or 11 rolls—usually double your money if 2 rolls, and triple your money if 12 rolls. However, you lose your money if a 5, 6, 7, or 8 rolls. It sounds like a good bet, but 20 of the 36 different dice combinations are not in the field, giving the house an edge of nearly 2.8%.

A friend of mine told me about this great system. He makes a $6 place bet on the 6 and 8, and a $5 bet on the 9. Then he bets $5 in the field. He says the only way he can lose is if the shooter rolls a 7, but he wins money on every other number.

Yes, but what does he win? If a 6 rolls, he loses his $5 field bet and gets paid $7 for his place bet, so all he actually won was $2. If a 7 rolls, he loses $22! The next time your friend tells you about this system, ask him why he's still working for a living.

What's the biggest mistake most players make at the dice table?

Not taking odds on pass line or come bets. If you don't take odds, you only get paid even money—no matter what the point is. By taking odds, you get paid the true amount.

Another mistake is betting back your winnings on the pass line. Stick with the minimum pass line bet until you're comfortably ahead, but always take as much odds as the casino will give you.

What is a buy bet?

At the dice table, you can buy a number and get paid the true odds. For example, a place bet on the 4 or 10 pays 9 to 5, but if you buy the 4 or 10 you get paid 2 to 1. In order to buy a number, however, you must pay a 5% commission. Consequently, it's only worth buying a number if you're betting at least $20. For lesser amounts, you'll get the same payoff whether you buy or place the number. When it's to your advantage to buy a number, the dealer will tell you.

What is a hop bet?

A hop bet is a next-roll bet on any dice combination. A hop bet on any double (4-4, 5-5, etc.) pays 31 for 1 in most casinos. Any other hop bet (such as 3-2 or 6-4) pays 16 for 1.

What are all those circled Cs and Es that I see in the middle of the dice table?

The "C" stands for craps and the "E" stands for 11. In other words, you're betting the next roll will be either craps or 11. The reason for all the circles is so the stickman can place your bet corresponding to your position at the table.

Some casinos offer double odds and some casinos offer 20X odds. Where should I play?

How much money are you willing to risk? Technically, you should take as much odds as you can get—because the casino has no advantage over you on the odds. Most casinos offer double odds, which means you can have up to double the amount of your pass line bet or come bet as odds. Other casinos (hoping to get your business) offer 10X odds, or even 100X odds! Statistically, for every $100 bet on the pass or come line by a person taking full 20X odds, the casino will win approximately 9.86¢. By taking 100X odds, it's only 2¢—but remember every time you lose you're out $10,100. (Thanks to Frank Scoblete, author of *Beat the Craps Out of the Casinos*, for these figures.)

Sometimes the dealer asks me to place another dollar on my odds. Is that a bet for him?

No, he's just giving you a better bet. Odds on the 5 and 9 pay 3-2. If you bet $5, and only take $5 odds, you should get back $7.50. But you'll only get back $7, unless it's a quarter dice table. By taking $6 odds, you'll get back $9, which are the true odds. An easy way to remember this rule is to always take an even amount of odds on an odd number (5 or 9).

Can I take odds on somebody else's bet?

If another player doesn't take odds, it's usually permissible for you to take odds on his bet—as long as you ask that player first.

Can I bet on the pass line or don't pass after the shooter has a point?

You must bet on the don't pass before the shooter rolls the dice, but you can bet on the pass line at any time. With casinos now offering as much as 100X odds, this is becoming a popular wager. In fact, there's even a name for it. It's called a "put bet," because you're literally putting a bet on the pass line or on any other number after the shooter already has a point. In casinos which offer 100X odds, you can place the minimum bet on the pass line or on another number, and then get paid the true odds for 100 times that amount. This lowers the house edge from 1.4% to 0.09%.

There is a drawback, however. By not betting the initial roll on the pass line or the come, you don't get paid for a 7 or 11. Consequently, you're giving up eight combinations out of 36 to win on the next roll.

Can I bet on the don't pass when I'm shooting the dice?

Sure. In fact, I saw a man do it once in 1943. Technically, you're not betting against yourself. You're betting against the dice.

How is the shooter determined at the dice table?

The dice go clockwise around the table, and everybody gets a chance to shoot. The shooter loses the dice by rolling a loser 7 before making his point number.

You don't have to shoot the dice, but most people do. It's part of the game's charm and "makes the game a physical thing," as Horseshoe owner Benny Binion used to say. Besides, you might roll a big hand, and somebody may give you something. At Caesars Palace, a woman betting $5 on the pass line rolled four hardways (doubles). Every time she rolled one, another player (who was betting $1,000 on each hardway) tossed her a $500 chip. So do you want to shoot the dice? I thought so.

Can I quit shooting the dice anytime I want?

Yes, but if you're shooting the dice, you're probably winning. And if you're winning, why would you want to stop? In rare instances where this happens, the dice will go to the next shooter who will finish the hand. Then the same shooter gets another turn for his own hand.

What is the proper etiquette when shooting the dice?

Never cup the dice in both hands, but use only one hand to shoot. Shoot from your position at the table. If you need more room, ask the players around you to move back a little. They won't mind, especially if you're rolling lots of numbers. Keep the dice in plain view at all times, and never grind them together. Always try to reach the other end of the table when throwing the dice. Other than that, you can do just about anything with the dice. You can blow on them; you can shake them as hard as you want; you can even set them on certain numbers before you shoot.

One so-called craps expert says he sets the dice with the three-spots in a "V" formation with his index and middle finger at the bottom of the "V" and his thumb at the top, then gently lobs them with as small an arc as possible. In my opinion, this isn't going to change the way the dice land, but at least the other players think you know what you're doing.

A little old lady was standing at the end of the crap table watching the action when the shooter accidentally threw both dice off the table. Kidding around, the floor supervisor asked the woman in a stern voice, "Madam, did you take the dice?"

With a sheepish look, the woman replied, "No sir, I'm sorry, I only took two ashtrays."

How can I bet the next roll will be a 7?

There's a one-roll proposition bet called "any seven," and you can bet it anytime you wish. Remember, though, that the odds of a 7 rolling are 6 to 1, and the bet only pays 4 to 1.

If you must make this bet during the middle of a hand, use the code phrase "big red." The dealers know you're betting on 7—and the other players don't!

How does the dealer keep up with everybody's bets?

The dealer places your come bets and place bets

according to your position at the table. The stickman does the same with any proposition bets that you make. So let them know if you decide to move to another spot at the table while you've got money in action. That way, no one else will get your money.

Do I have to tell the dealer every time I make a bet?

You don't have to tell the dealer if you're making any bet that's printed on the table: pass line, don't pass, come, don't come, field, Big 6, Big 8. However, if you want odds on your come or don't come bets, of if you wish to place a number, then you must tell the dealer. On proposition bets, toss your money to the stickman and tell him what you want.

What is the Big 6 and Big 8?

When you bet on the Big 6 or Big 8, you're betting that either a 6 or 8 will roll before a 7. These bets only pay you even money, regardless of how much your wager is, which gives the house an advantage of 9.09%. You're much better off to place the 6 or 8. That way, you get $7 back for each $6 you bet.

What is a horn bet?

It's a bet covering four different propositions on the next roll of the dice: 2, 3, 11, and 12. This is one of the worst bets on the table, so don't waste your money on it. Equally as bad is a world bet, which covers the same four numbers plus 7.

When can I remove my money at the dice table?

As soon as you're paid. You can also remove any bet at any time except your original pass line bet and your original come bet (once point numbers are established).

However, you can remove your odds on pass line and come bets any time you wish.

If you're betting on the don't pass or don't come, you can remove your original bet at any time—because once the shooter establishes a point the odds are now in your favor. Remember, though, anytime the casino allows you to remove your bet . . . you don't want to!

How many people can play at the table?

On most dice tables there are eight chip compartments on each end of the rail, so technically there's room for eight players on either end. The other players will usually make room for a couple of more, so figure on a maximum of ten players on each end. If no one will let you near the table, then flash a roll of $100 bills at the dealer. He'll get you in.

How many people work at the table?

There are four dealers on each crew, with one on break at any given moment. Generally, each dealer works 20 minutes on the stick, and then 40 minutes on a base before taking a 20-minute break. You might also notice a person seated at the table. This is the boxman, whose job is to supervise payoffs, settle disputes, and kill anybody who gets out of line.

I notice that a lot of players bet "any craps" on the first roll. If the shooter rolls a craps, they lose their pass line bet but they get paid 8 for 1 for any craps. Isn't that a good idea?

No. There are 36 combinations on the dice, and only four ways to roll a craps (2, 3, 12). If a craps rolls, you should get back 9 to 1. The payoff is only 8 for 1, or 7 to 1. It's just not worth it.

Why do the hard 6 and 8 (two 3s or two 4s) pay 10 for 1 while the hard 4 and 10 only pay 8 for 1?

There are four ways to roll an easy 6 or 8, and only two ways to roll an easy 4 or 10. Since it's easier to lose your hardway bets on 6 and 8, they pay a little more.

Be careful betting the hardways. The house advantage on the hard 4 and 10 is 11%, and it's 9% on the hard 6 and 8. This compares with a house edge of only 1.4% on the pass line with odds, and 1.6% on 6 and 8 place bets.

If the minimum bet at the table is $5, does that mean each bet has to be $5?

Most casinos will allow you to bet as little as $1 on any single proposition bet, even on a $5 table.

Why does the stickman say "Yo-leven" instead of "Eleven"?

Because he's from Philadelphia. No, it's because 7 and 11 sound alike. By saying "Yo-leven" he's letting everyone know it wasn't a 7 that rolled—but a "Yo-leven." Consequently, "yo" has become a slang expression for 11. So if you ever hear somebody say, "Give me a dollar on yo," it just means that player is betting a dollar on 11.

Why isn't the game of craps as popular as it used to be?

A brief history lesson might be in order. World War II was grinding to a close. G.I.'s were coming home, and after stomping around Paris and Rome they found that life in suburban Americana was bor-r-r-ing. So they began flocking to Vegas by the thousands, shooting craps like they did aboard battleships and in Army barracks. With the end of the post-war boom, however, the game began a slow spiral into oblivion. Its recent resurgence is due mainly to the proliferation of books on the subject, and the fact that it's the most exciting game in the casino.

Why is the game called craps?

A much simpler form of the game, called "crabs," was brought to New Orleans in the middle of the 19th century by the French. Legend has it that the dots on the dice looked like the eyes of a crab. The Americans misunderstood the name of it, and started calling it craps. Hey, it could have been worse!

Can the casino legally change the dice in the middle of a hand?

Yes, but everybody would scream their heads off. Of course, that doesn't mean it's never been done. When Morris Shenker was running the old Dunes Hotel, a New York junket was winning big at one of the dice tables. Shenker came downstairs in his bathrobe (he lived in the hotel), and studied the dice carefully. Then he dropped them back on the table. Unfortunately, it wasn't the same pair of dice. Shenker had switched them with another pair in his pocket!

The new dice weren't loaded, or anything like that. Shenker was just hoping to change the players' luck by putting new dice on the table. (P.S. It didn't work.)

When Morris Shenker first bought the Dunes Hotel, he called a meeting to introduce himself to all the employees. After a short speech, he asked if anyone had any questions.

A dealer stood and asked, "I'd like to know why we don't have the same benefits that other hotel employees have."

Shenker replied, "That shouldn't concern you. You don't work here anymore."

Can I ask for different dice when I'm shooting?

Sure, you can change dice as often as you want. It'll drive the other players crazy, but it's your prerogative. You can also ask for the same dice if you accidentally throw one of them off the table.

At a downtown casino in Las Vegas, I saw a dice table the size of an airport runway. Why aren't all dice tables the same size?

Dice tables come in sizes of 10, 12, and 14 feet. Most players like the smaller tables because the game doesn't get as crowded. Casinos also prefer the smaller tables for the same reason. If someone rolls a big hand at a smaller table, the casino doesn't lose as much money because there are fewer people playing.

Where does the casino get its dice, and how are they made?

Casinos order dice in lots from gaming supply houses such as the Bud Jones Company or Paul-Son. The dice are cut from sheets of acrylic plastic and then sanded down into cubes that are usually five-eighths of an inch in size. Spots for the numbers are drilled by a micrometer, and a syringe fills the holes with a plastic paint that's exactly the same weight as the material it replaced. Finally, each lot of dice is inscribed with the casino's logo, a sequence of numbers, and whatever special markings the casino requests.

What is "Crapless Craps"?

The Stratosphere offers this game, which is just like regular craps except you don't lose your pass line bet if the shooter's first roll is a craps (2, 3, 12). Instead, that becomes the point, and the shooter has to roll it again before rolling a 7. The problem with this game is that if the shooter rolls an 11 on the first roll, it doesn't win like it would in the regular game. Eleven now becomes the shooter's point, and he has to roll another 11 before rolling a 7—which he won't do two out of three times. Consequently, the house edge at crapless craps is a whopping 5.38%. Stick with the regular game.

What was the longest dice hand on record?

That's a hard question to answer, because no one has ever timed a hand from the moment the shooter first picked up the dice. After all, if a 7 is supposed to roll once every six rolls, how long can a dice hand last? Of course, that's what makes the game so intriguing—the idea that somebody's going to pick up those dice and roll them forever. It never happens, but there have been documented instances of some unusually long rolls. At the California Club in downtown Las Vegas, a player named Stanley Fujitake shot the dice for three hours and six minutes. The 1989 hand started at 1:30 in the morning and lasted until 4:36 a.m. Fujitake threw the dice 118 times for 18 pass line winners, which cost the casino an estimated $750,000. Other notable rolls include a 28-pass hand at the Desert Inn in 1951, and a 32-pass hand at the Sahara in 1982.

Newspaper reporter Bill Slocum witnessed the following hand at Harrah's at Lake Tahoe on March 18, 1961, and wrote about it later in the *New York Mirror*.

"Nothing very interesting about him really. Except that he didn't know what the hell he was doing. Wasn't drunk, or anything like that. He just stood there throwing the dice, his face going stiffer and stiffer as his luck continued."

The roll only lasted 37 minutes, which is about how long the average gambler waits for a cocktail waitress. But in that short period of time the "miracle shooter" (as

Slocum described him) rolled 32 consecutive winners, including seven straight sevens.

How many pairs of dice are being thrown in Las Vegas casinos at any given moment?

As I write this, approximately 5,400 pairs of dice are bouncing down the crap tables right now. Let's see if we can get a rundown on the numbers that rolled.   Yes, they're coming in on the tickertape right now. One hard 6, fifteen 11s, three easy 4s, five easy 8s, six 9s, six 5s, one 12, and 5,363 loser 7s.

5
Roulette

How much does a roulette wheel cost?

Around $10,000, but that includes the magnet and the foot brake. (Just kidding.)

How often is the roulette ball replaced?

The only time the ball is replaced is when it becomes worn or "out of round," which hardly ever happens. Most casinos supply the roulette dealer with two balls, one slightly larger than the other. Some dealers like the feel of a larger roulette ball. Another reason for two balls at the roulette table is so the ball can be changed if a good player requests it. (Yes, this happens all the time.)

Where did the game of roulette originate?

It's one of the oldest games in the world. Origins go back to ancient Greece, when soldiers would spin their shields on the points of their swords and then bet on where they stopped. In Roman times, it's said that Caesar himself played a form of roulette on a chariot wheel in the palace game room. The French refined the game early in the 19th century, gave it the fancy name of roulette (little wheel), and it's been a casino mainstay ever since.

At what point do I make my bets at the roulette table?

After the dealer has paid all bets and removed the point marker. You can continue to bet even after the dealer spins the ball for the next game. When the ball begins to slow down, the dealer will wave his hand over the table and announce, "No more bets."

What are some of the different bets I can make at roulette?

Any wager outside the 36 number-layout is called an "outside bet." Notice the six boxes on the edge of the layout closest to you:

"1 to 18"   "18 to 36"
"Odd"   "Even"
"Red"   "Black"

You're covering 18 numbers on each of these bets, and your payoff is even money.

By betting inside the square marked "1st 12," you're covering the first 12 numbers on the wheel. This pays 2-1. Payoffs are the same for the squares marked "2nd 12" and "3rd 12." You may also make what is called a "column" bet. Now you're betting any number in a column of 12 numbers, and again your payoff is 2-1.

"Inside bets" are wagers on individual numbers, and there are many different ways to play these numbers.

- **Straight bet** is a wager on one number, and pays 35-1.

- **Split bet** is a wager on two numbers, and pays 17-1.

- **Street bet** is a wager on a group of three numbers, and pays 11-1.

- **Corner bet** is a wager on four numbers, and pays 8-1.

- **First Five** is a wager on 0, 00, 1, 2, and 3, and pays 6-1. This bet is not available on single-zero wheels.

* **Line bet** is a wager on a grouping of six numbers, and pays 5-1.

What is the worst bet on the roulette wheel?

Betting on the first five numbers (0, 00, 1, 2, and 3). The house edge on this bet is 7.89%, compared with 5.2% on all other bets.

According to a veteran roulette dealer, there's a way to lower the house edge on this bet to 5.2%. Instead of betting one chip on the five numbers, make a split bet on 0 and 00 with one chip and a street bet (three-number bet) on 1, 2, and 3 with another chip. Instead of getting back 6-1, you'll get 17-1 if 0 or 00 shows, and 11-1 if 1, 2, or 3 shows. You've invested two chips instead of one, but you'll pick up an extra eleven chips if 0 or 00 shows, and lose only one chip if 1, 2, or 3 comes up.

How are my winnings paid?

On outside bets, each wager is paid individually. On inside bets, your payoff is usually totaled, and all your winnings are shoved to you in one big beautiful stack of chips.

Why is there a compass at some roulette wheels?

It's a precaution to ensure that nobody has switched the plastic ball for one with a metal insert that could make it possible to rig the ball to land in a certain section on the roulette wheel. Whenever a dealer is relieved at the roulette game, the new dealer's first responsibility is to place the ball on the compass. If the needle moves, so does the gun in the security guard's holster.

Does the dealer spin the ball in the same direction as the wheel is spinning?

No, the ball is spun in the opposite direction. On a left-handed wheel (a table with the wheel on the left-hand side), the wheel is spun clockwise and the ball counter-clockwise. On a right-handed table, it's just the opposite.

Why aren't the numbers on a roulette wheel in numerical order?

Let's stop the wheel and take a look at it. Excuse me, folks, this'll only take a second. The roulette wheel is designed so that each spin is completely random. Therefore, a red number will always be next to a black number, number 1 will be directly opposite number 2, 27 will be opposite 28, and so on. There are no more than two even numbers grouped together, and no more than two odd numbers. On a double-zero wheel the configuration will be slightly different. Thanks, everybody. You can get back to your game now.

How much do all the numbers on the roulette wheel add up to?

Shades of *The Exorcist*! The numbers on the roulette wheel add up to 666. (Yeah, but does that include the zero and double zero?)

Why is there no dollar value on roulette chips?

Unlike other games in the casino, you have the option at roulette to make your chips worth any amount up to the house limit. Unless otherwise specified, roulette chips are usually worth 25¢ or $1, depending on where you play. Some players, however, like to play for higher stakes. So a chip the same color as theirs will be placed by the side of the wheel, with a button on top signifying how much each chip is worth. You could be betting a dollar, and the person next to you could be betting as much as $5,000. You'll never know, and neither will the I.R.S.

If the minimum bet at roulette is $5, does that mean every bet I make has to be $5?

On a $5 minimum table, each outside bet must be at least $5. On the inside bets, where you're betting on individual numbers, you can make $1 bets—as long as your total wager is $5.

What is the lighted board I see at some roulette tables?

It's called a reader board, and it shows the last series of numbers that have come up on the roulette wheel. Since roulette is strictly a game of chance, these numbers don't mean anything. Still, it's a convenience by the casino for players who like to track the winning numbers.

Why do some roulette tables have a single zero while others have a zero and a double zero?

Playing at a single-zero table gives the casino a 2.6% advantage. With two zeros, the house edge doubles to 5.2%. So you figure it out. You can find single zero roulette tables in Vegas at the Stratosphere and Monte Carlo. Other casinos may have single-zero wheels, but the minimum bet is usually higher.

In defense of American casinos, operators have tried to popularize roulette by offering single-zero wheels, but most players don't seem to care how many zeros are on the wheel. They'll go where the other players go. One Las Vegas casino put a single-zero wheel right next to a double-zero wheel, and guess where all the players were? They were all at the double-zero wheel! Not one of them noticed the difference.

What does "en prison" mean?

My brother-in-law can answer that better than I can. Oh, you mean at roulette! It's an option available in some foreign countries (such as England and Atlantic City) whereby you get a second chance for your money if you bet on any even-money payoff (red or black, odd or even, first 18 numbers or last 18 numbers) and the roulette ball lands on zero. Then your bet is "en prison" until the next spin of the wheel. If a black number shows on the next spin, your original bet is returned to you. If a red number shows, you lose your bet. This cuts the house edge by about 1%.

What is a "neighbors" bet?

It's a bet on one number and the two numbers on either side of that number. For example, these five numbers are next to one another on the wheel: 36, 24, 3, 15, and 34. To make a neighbors bet on these numbers, place your money on the table and tell the dealer, "Give me 3 and the neighbors." If any of the five numbers in that cluster come up on the next spin, you get paid 35-1. Since you're betting five numbers, however, you have to bet the table minimum on each number.

What is a "snake" bet?

This is a roulette wager that goes all the way back to the days of the Wild West saloons. It's hard to find nowadays, but it's a bet on all the connecting red numbers which form a zig zag pattern across the table (1, 5, 9, 12, 14, 16, 19, 23, 27, 30, 32, and 34). It's a 12-number bet, and pays 2-1.

What is the record for the most black or red numbers in a row?

Nobody knows, but a roulette dealer at Foxwood's in Connecticut said that he counted 16 red numbers in a row. Not to be outdone, a dealer at New York-New York in Las Vegas reported black coming up 19 times in a row! It is said that an English lord once won 17 consecutive bets on black while betting the maximum in Monte Carlo. He then retired to the English countryside and never gambled again. That's the story anyway.

What are the odds of the same number coming up twice in a row?

That's a tricky question, and there are two different answers. Here's the first one. Let's say a friend of yours tells you to bet on 23, and if it comes up to bet all the winnings on 23 to repeat. The odds of that happening are 1,444-1. This is based on multiplying 38 X 38, since there are 38 numbers on the wheel.

Now let's say that when you walk up to the table the ball has just landed on 23. If you bet on it again, the odds of it repeating are 38-1, because the first spin becomes irrelevant. The only thing that matters now is the next spin, and the odds of 23 repeating are still 38-1.

True Story

At Caesars Palace, on July 14, 2000, at 1:35 p.m., the number 7 came up six times in a row on Roulette Wheel #211. To figure the odds of such an occurrence, multiply 38 X 38 X 38 X 38 X 38 X 38, or THREE BILLION TO ONE! The dealer said it was the first time he had seen this in his 27-year career. And no wonder. The only other recorded instance of this happening was on July 9, 1959 at El San Juan Hotel in Puerto Rico, when the number 10 came up six times in succession.

Another sidelight. After the ball landed on 7 four times, the floor supervisor told the pit boss, "I'll bet you a million dollars that it won't come up again." Then here it came again, and again.

How much money did the table lose? A whopping $300.

What is the most popular number on the roulette wheel?

Number 17, and there are two reasons why. It's right in the center of the layout, and it's the number that James Bond bets in the movies. Well, he never loses, does he?

An Asian high roller walked up to a roulette table with two stacks of $25,000 chips—a million dollars in all. On his first bet, he won $300,000! After the dealer paid him, the man shoved 19 $100 chips in front of the dealer, saying something in Chinese which the dealer didn't understand. The dealer looked at the man questioningly, and the man repeated what he said before.

The dealer finally asked, "For me?" The man didn't reply, so the dealer put the 19 $100 chips in his pocket, figuring it was a tip.

The man sat there for a moment, a grim look on his face, and then shoved 19 more $100 chips in front of the dealer. Then he screamed in English, "PUT—MONEY—ON NUMBER—TWO!"

6
Baccarat

Why do people keep score while playing baccarat?

They're tracking the hands, in hopes they may spot some pattern in the way the cards are falling. Remember, though, that eight decks of cards are used in baccarat. Consequently, each hand is independent of all the others. Baccarat is strictly a guessing game, and keeping score isn't going to change anything.

Here's another interesting fact. In larger casinos, where big bets are an everyday occurrence, the casino will usually use brand new cards every time the shoe is emptied. This guards against any improprieties by either the players or casino employees—and because the players sometimes mutilate the cards when they deal them from the shoe.

The dealer will shuffle all eight decks, then offer them to a player to cut. Now the dealer turns over the first card, and it's a 9. The dealer will then deal nine more cards face down, and these will go into the discard rack. The rest of the cards will be placed in the shoe, and the game gets underway.

Where did the game of baccarat originate?

Its roots go back to Rome over five centuries ago. Other games such as Punto Banco and Chemin de Fer are nothing more than variations of this ancient game. There's an interesting story as to how baccarat came to be. It seemed that everyone in Rome loved to gamble, but the emperor couldn't figure out any of the games. He told his court advisors to come up with a simple game that even he could play. Hence baccarat, where all you're doing is guessing which hand will be closer to 9: the player's hand or the banker's hand.

Incidentally, baccarat was brought to Las Vegas from Havana in 1959 by John Scarne and Tommy Ronzoni. It was first played in the Deuville Room at the old Sands Hotel. A novelty game at first, it's now found at every major Vegas resort.

Didn't the casinos use paper money at one time in Vegas baccarat rooms?

Yes, paper money was used until the mid-seventies, which made baccarat even more glamorous. The money (ironed every night so the bills would stay crisp) was bet in neat stacks, and crowds would watch as the stacks of money changed hands—usually from the players to the casino. But the process of counting the bills after each hand delayed the game so much that the casinos began using chips. Now the game is much faster—and not nearly as exciting.

Am I betting with the casino when I bet on the banker?

No, the casino is merely fading your action, no matter where you bet. It's almost a 50-50 proposition, so the casino makes its money by charging a 5% commission on winning banker hands. Taking that commission into account, the house edge on banker bets is 1.06%. On player bets, the house edge is 1.24%.

If the house edge is lower on the banker, wouldn't it be wise to bet on the banker all the time?

Some players do, but in the long run it just won't work. Baccarat is a guessing game, much like flipping a coin. You've got to be lucky (and it helps to be rich).

Can I bet the hand ends in a tie?

Yes, it's the only proposition bet on the table, and a bad one at that. In the event the hand ends in a tie, you are paid 8-1. Statistically, a tie comes up once every 10.5 hands, giving the house a 14.4% advantage. Enough said?

Are there any strategies I can use at baccarat?

Many experts are convinced that baccarat is a game of streaks, and that taking advantage of these streaks is the best way to beat the game. One so-called expert says you should watch the first hand, bet the next round on the winner of the first hand, then bet progressively if the steak continues. Then he goes on to say that if this doesn't work, then wait for a streak to occur and bet the *other* way. (And this guy's an expert?)

If baccarat is such a great game, why don't more people play it?

Because it's intimidating. Let's face it, who wants to play a game where the dealers are dressed better than the customers? A recent survey showed that only 1% of casino patrons play baccarat, and that's why mini-baccarat was introduced. You can play the mini-version for as little as $5 in some casinos.

I notice that the players get to deal the cards at baccarat. It looks complicated.

This is part of the European charm of the game. Here you are in Vegas, everyone's watching you with eager anticipation, the tension mounts as you slowly slide the cards out of the shoe, flipping them nonchalantly to the croupier. Let's face it, you are one classy guy! So don't

let the dealing part of the game scare you. The dealer—
er, croupier—will tell you what to do.

How do I pay my commission in baccarat?

In regular baccarat, the dealer keeps up with your
commission by using marker buttons. When the shoe is
completed, each player's commissions are settled. In mini-
baccarat, the commissions are usually paid after each
hand.

Is there an easy way to figure my commission?

Here's how the dealers do it. Divide the winning bet
by two, then subtract a zero.

For example, you make an $80 bet on the Banker and
win. Half of 80 is 40, subtract the zero, and your 5%
commission is $4.

What is a natural?

At baccarat, a natural is a total of 8 or 9 on either the
player's first two cards or the banker's first two cards. In
the event of a natural, no more cards are dealt.

What is a monkey?

A monkey is a slang expression for a ten or face card.
It's very rarely used by civilized gamblers—which is why
you hear it so often in Las Vegas.

Do I have to play every hand?

You don't have to play every hand at any casino game.
If the dealer asks you to make a bet, simply tell him you're
sitting out that particular hand. Then ask him, "Where the
heck is the cocktail waitress?"

7
Keno

When I play keno, I notice the word "aggregate" on the list of payoffs. What does that mean?

It means the total payoff (usually $50,000 a game) is divided proportionately among all the winners. So if you hit an 8-spot for $50,000 (i.e., pick 8 numbers out of the 20 drawn in the game) and someone else hits a 7-spot for $21,000, the win will be divided proportionately. Then subtract another one-third for federal taxes, plus a big tip for the keno runner and another tip for the ticket writer, and that leaves you with . . . enough to play another game of keno.

What are the odds of hitting an 8-spot keno ticket?

The odds of catching all eight numbers on an 8-spot are 230,114 to 1. How often does somebody hit one of these long shots? I asked two keno writers. One of them, who had been a keno writer for 23 years, has never seen it happen. The other, a keno writer for 27 years, said, "More than one, less than five." One of those who did was "so drunk he couldn't stand up," she said, "but he did give me a $1,000 tip when he found out he won $25,000." By the way, the man's winning numbers were 1, 12, 21, 32, 41, 52, 61, and 72.

The following true story will give you an idea on how tough it is to beat the game of keno. In 1962, a crooked keno manager joined forces with a shady customer in a downtown Vegas casino. He rigged 20 of the 80 keno balls so they wouldn't get sucked up the tube when the balls were being drawn. Now only 60 balls were being used in each game, making it a lot easier to parlay a 35¢ keno ticket into a $10,000 jackpot—which was the top prize at the time.

Before the two were caught, they spent $4,000 of their own money, and never did hit an 8-spot. And that was using 60 balls, instead of 80!

How many numbers should I play on a keno ticket?

If you want to win the big money (and that's what keno is all about), avoid betting less than five numbers. A $5 four-spot pays $625; a $5 five-spot pays $3,750. As one long-time Vegas keno writer explained to me: "Because only one-fourth of the balls are drawn, you only have a 25% chance of hitting any number. So since you're taking a chance in the first place, at least give yourself a chance to win something."

How do I mark my keno ticket?

Blank tickets and crayons are supplied by the casino. Your ticket will not be accepted if you use ink, pencils, scorpion venom, or bat's blood.

Do I have to write a new keno ticket for each game?

Yes, unless you're playing the same numbers. In that case, just present your old ticket to the keno writer, and she'll give you a new one. Since keno is strictly a guessing game (and a long shot at that), I recommend playing the same numbers all the time. Or put it this way. What if you pick eight new numbers, and your eight old numbers come up in the next game? Now you know why the suicide rate is so high in Nevada.

What is a "Quick Pick"?

This is a keno ticket where the computer picks your numbers. In other words, the computer picks the numbers while the casino picks your pocket.

Why would anyone play keno if it's such a bad bet?

It's the idea of winning a lot of money off a small bet. The average game, from start to finish, is about 10 to 15 minutes. So if you're playing a $2 keno ticket in each game, it's only costing you about $10 an hour, with the outside chance of collecting fifty grand. Meanwhile, most of the people at the blackjack tables are losing $10 every hand!

If I win at keno, how long do I have to collect my money?

Before the start of the next game, which gives you about 10 minutes. The exception is if you play 21 games or more (up to 1,000) on what is known as a "Multi-Game" ticket. Then you have one year to collect your winnings.

Where did keno originate?

It was originally called "Chinese Lottery," and was played in the Far East over 3,000 years ago. In fact, the Great Wall of China is said to have been financed by this game. Using Chinese characters painted on maple balls, it was brought to the United States by immigrants at the turn of the century. Gaming pioneer Warren Nelson changed the Chinese characters to names of famous race horses, and introduced the game to Nevada as Race Horse Keno. In 1951, numbers were substituted for the horses' names, and the game became keno.

What are some of the different tickets I can play?

The most popular is the straight ticket, where you play any combination of 1 to 20 numbers. Others include:

Split ticket, where you split your numbers into two or more groups.

Way ticket, with at least three groups of equal numbers.

Combination ticket, where you divide your numbers into equal or unequal groups.

King ticket, where one number is used with other combinations to make a special combination ticket.

The keno writer will help you with any of these tickets.

Should I use a keno runner?

Many people play keno while eating in a casino, and in that case I would definitely use the services of a keno runner. Otherwise, play in the keno lounge. Drinks are free, and there's always something exciting going on. Look! A man just dropped a bucket of nickels on the floor! Look! Someone just hit two numbers on an eight-spot! Look! That woman sleeping in the next chair looks just like Aunt Harriet! Yes, the excitement never stops.

If you use a keno runner, it's still your responsibility to present your winning ticket before the next game starts. That's why it never hurts to "case the joint" before you play. That way, you can get to the main keno counter as quickly as possible—just in case you finally win something.

8
Sports Betting

Who sets the lines on sporting events?

Betting lines are set by professional oddsmakers, and adjusted according to the volume of betting on either team. The line can fluctuate from day to day, so shop around when making your bets. (And never make a bet just because the game's on TV.)

Is the line the same in every sports book?

No. A few big bets in one book can make the line move by several points. Meanwhile, the line may not have changed in another book, where no big bets were made. This won't happen too often because all major sports books are connected by computer, so each one knows what the line is in other casinos at any given moment—and consequently may adjust their lines accordingly in hopes of keeping the action split equally on both sides.

The computer readout will look like this:

```
                Caesars  Mirage  Stardust  MGM  Hilton  Bally's
NCAAB
2/18  8:00 ET
  HOUSTON----
  CINCINNATI
                 22.0    22.5     22.0    21.5   22.0   22.0
```

(The dashes show that Houston is favored by anywhere from 21.5 to 22.5 points, depending on the book.)

The home team is always on the bottom, so they're playing at Cincinnati.

What is a "middled" bet?

That's when you find yourself in the enviable position of being in the middle: by betting the favorite when the line first opens, then betting the other team if the point spread (or line) moves dramatically. For example, San Francisco opens at -8 over San Diego, and you bet San Francisco. Early betting is on San Francisco, so the sports book moves the line to -12. Now you bet San Diego at +12. San Francisco wins 24-14. You've won both bets, and you've "middled" the casino!

What is the difference between a parlay and a teaser?

On a parlay ticket, you're combining two or more games on one bet, and betting the point spread. On a teaser, the sports book allows you to move the line a few points, thus making your multi-game bet a little safer. Consequently, you get a lower payback on a teaser.

Disadvantage of either one: You have to win every single game on your ticket.   One loser, and you're out of the money UNLESS you bet a two-team parlay or teaser and one game ends in a tie. In that case, *all* your money will be refunded, even if you already lost the other game. (A tie in a three or more team parlay reduces your bet to the next lowest betting bracket.)

What is a money line?

Since baseball is not a high-scoring game like football or basketball, the sports book uses a money line instead of a point spread. Here's how a money line works. If a team is favored by 7 to 5 odds, that means you have to bet $70 to win $50. It won't read that way on the board.

Instead, it will read: "New York -140." Translation: New York is favored, and you have to bet $140 to win $100, $70 to win $50, or $7 to win $5.

What is a run line?

A relatively new bet in baseball, the run line lists the number of runs the favorite team should win by. Example: Chicago is favored, and the run line is -1.5. If Chicago wins by two runs or more, you get paid if you take Chicago. If you take the other side, you can lose by one run and still win your bet. The run line automatically uses listed pitchers. If the pitchers are changed, all bets are off.

How does the sports book make its money on football and basketball?

In any game based on a point spread, you have to pay a 10% vigorish or commission on each ticket. So if you make a $20 bet on your favorite team, you have to bet $22 to win $20. The sports book is hoping, of course, that half the bettors will take the favorite and half will take the underdog, so it's going to earn around 5% no matter who wins.

What are the most popular sports events for a sports book?

The Super Bowl is far and away the most popular event of the year, with more than $50 million bet each year at Nevada's legal books. This is followed by the NCAA college basketball playoffs and the World Series. From a gambler's standpoint, the most popular sporting events in order are professional football, college football, professional baseball, professional basketball, and college basketball.

Should I use a professional handicapper?

I wouldn't. A good handicapper will usually charge you up to $20 and more for a pick. Unfortunately, professionals book losers just like the rest of us. And if you lose, you've lost your money plus the money you paid the handicapper!

Most sports books offer a battery of proposition bets on major events like the Super Bowl, such as which team will win the coin toss, which team will score the first field goal, which quarterback will complete the most passes, and so on. Stay away from these, and bet this game like you'd bet any other. You'll be money ahead in the long run.

Can I make a bet on the presidential election?

You usually can't make a bet on any event in which a vote is necessary to determine the winner. So that lets out political elections, the Academy Awards, the number one ranking in college football or basketball, Most Valuable Player Awards, Heisman Trophy winner, and the date of Willie Nelson's next I.R.S. hearing.

How about boxing matches?

Sure, but let me ask you this. When's the last time you saw a boxing match that didn't leave you feeling like you got cheated afterwards? Remember when Gerry Cooney fought Larry Holmes? Cooney went down twice—and that was during the weigh-in!

If you really want to give your money away, though, here's how the bet will look on the board:

            HOLMES   -300
            COONEY   +200

This means that Holmes is a 3 to 1 favorite, so you have to lay $300 to win $100 on Holmes, or (if you're like me) $30 to win $10. Meanwhile, you would bet $100 to win $200 if you took Cooney.

In the event of a draw, all money is refunded.

How long do I have to collect my winning sports bet?

Usually 60 days from the date of the event. If you live out of town, you can either send me the ticket and I'll collect your winnings for you—or you can mail your ticket and the casino will send you a check. This information is printed on the reverse side of your ticket.

Do I have to pay taxes on winning sports bets?

In parimutuel pools, your winnings are subject to withholding taxes—but only if the winnings are at least 300 times the size of the amount bet. This includes anything over $600 on a $2 bet. I wouldn't worry about it too much, though. One sports book writer told me he's only paid one winner on this kind of bet in the last four years.

All is not lost even if you hit a 300-1 longshot. Remember, you can deduct your gambling losses from your winnings. You'll have to itemize these deductions on Schedule A of your income tax return. You can do this by holding on to losing tickets or by requesting a "win/loss statement" from your favorite casino. Allow 3 to 4 weeks for the report (and another 3 to 4 weeks for an audit by the I.R.S.).

Why can't I use a cellular telephone in a sports book?

You might be calling someone in another state to let them know what the line is on a sporting event. Technically it's illegal to gamble or transmit gambling information across state lines. Casinos are also restricted by law from connecting you to any sports book by telephone.

9
Crime and
Punishment

Can a casino legally bar a card counter?

Technically, a casino is considered private property, and therefore can evict anyone from the premises for any reason. This includes card counters, underage gamblers, shirtless men (and women), loud and obnoxious behavior, intoxication, panhandling, peddling, pandering, and prostitution.

Do the mobs still run Las Vegas?

How many times do I gotta told you, dere ain't no such ting as de mob. Today just about every resort in Las Vegas is owned and run by corporations, and everything's strictly legit.

The gambling industry is managed by the Nevada Gaming Commission and its enforcement arm known as the Gaming Control Board. The whole idea of mob control or mob influence is so abhorrent to Vegas' glittery family image that gaming overseers take every precaution to guard against it. To be licensed in Nevada today, any officer or prospective owner of a casino has to undergo a rigorous background check, and the casino or individual has to pay any expense incurred in that investigation.

One example that comes to mind occurred when Masao Nangaku bought the Dunes Hotel. He lived in Tokyo, and several investigators from the Control Board went there to delve into his financial and personal records. The resulting investigation took several months, and cost Nangaku over $1 million.

What is Nevada's Black Book?

The infamous "Black Book" is the list of persons banned from Nevada casinos by the Nevada Gaming Commission. Recent entries include Frank "Lefty" Rosenthal, a one-time mob overseer at the Stardust Hotel, and Ron Harris, who was caught trying to rig a jackpot on an Atlantic City casino slot machine. Harris should have known better. He was a former agent of the Atlantic City Gaming Control Board!

One alleged mobster showed up at his hearing dressed in a tuxedo. When questioned by gaming regulators as to his attire, he replied that he "had never been invited to join anything before and wanted to show the proper respect." He wound up in the Black Book anyway.

Why aren't there any monuments honoring Flamingo founder Bugsy Siegel?

Because he was a crook! In defense of Siegel, he was one of the city's gaming pioneers. His Flamingo Hotel, built in 1946, gave Las Vegas an aura of illegality, which was just what people wanted after five years of war, rationing, and Betty Grable movies. Due to cost overruns, Siegel and his underworld partners spent $5 million on the property, which was $4 million more than his partners expected. Rumors circulated that Siegel was siphoning off most of this cash, and the following year he was executed gangland-style at his girlfriend's home in Beverly Hills.

At one time, there were plans afoot to erect a monument honoring Siegel, but city fathers thought this would smear Las Vegas' new family image. However, there is a commemorative plaque honoring Siegel at the Flamingo, and it's located between the main casino and the pool area. Don't waste your time looking for Siegel's old suite. It was bulldozed several years ago to make room for more rooms and a bigger buffet. Even Bugsy couldn't stop progress.

What does the term "eye in the sky" mean?

The term "eye in the sky" refers to the early days of casino gambling, when surveillance people monitored the players and employees through two-way mirrors in the ceiling. Thanks to modern technology, casinos today use sophisticated surveillance equipment to record all the action. Next time you're in a casino, take a look overhead. Those black bubbles suspended from the ceiling house remote-control surveillance cameras. Operated by controls at the surveillance monitoring stations, these cameras can pan, tilt, and zoom in on any area of the casino. Others are stationary, and are trained on progressive slot machines, count rooms, and the cashier's cage. "They keep honest people honest," one surveillance chief said. Catching crooks is a bonus.

How much does a surveillance system cost?

Each major casino in Las Vegas spends from $1 to $2 million on surveillance equipment, and most of the cameras used today record everything in living color.

How often is the tape changed in surveillance video cameras?

The tapes are changed every eight hours, and are usually kept for a week before being reused.

Which Nevada casino was the first to use overhead surveillance equipment?

Bill Harrah of Harrah's in Reno began using two-way mirrors in 1946. The story goes that the casino manager suspected a scam on one of the games, and took Harrah to a crawl space in the attic so Harrah could see for himself. This gave Harrah the idea to keep observers in the attic at all times to watch the games, and other casinos quickly followed suit.

Harrah, by the way, was also the first in Nevada to carpet a casino and to use bells and whistles on slot machines. Gee, Bill, thanks a lot!

Do casinos still use shills?

At one time, shills (casino employees who pretend they're gambling to lure others to the tables) were used extensively by Las Vegas casinos. Unlawful in some states but still legal in Nevada, the use of shills isn't that prevalent any more. About the only place where you might still see shills are in some of the baccarat pits. These shills are easily recognized because they drink fake drinks, bet with fake chips, and wear fake furs, fake hairpieces, and fake diamonds.

What are some of the things people do to cheat casinos?

First, let me emphasize that 99% of casino customers are honest, law-abiding citizens. You have to remember, though, that a casino is like a bank. Large sums of money are handled daily in each casino, and there's always going

> *"One of the most common scams in Las Vegas is people breaking their own car window in a casino parking lot, and then reporting that merchandise was stolen from their cars. Some casinos will pay these claims on the spot to avoid bad publicity."*
>
> Hotel Security Guard

to be someone trying to get that money without working (or gambling) for it.

Slot machine cheats are one of the casino's biggest threats. Millions of dollars in gaming revenue are lost each year to slot thieves, who work alone or in packs. They're not afraid to take on any machine in any location, and usually have the latest electronic gadgetry as soon as a more sophisticated machine hits the market.

The biggest ploy used by slot thieves is putting counterfeit slugs or foreign coins in the machines. On average, nine tons of these are recovered from slot machines in Clark County each year at a cost to casinos of $20 million.

Here are other measures used by slot cheats:

Stringing—Using a string or piece of wire attached to a coin through a small hole to "yo yo" the coin until it triggers the machine's coin-acceptance switch.

Magnet—Using a magnet on older slot machines to line up the jackpot reels. A cheat places a magnet on the side of the machine, which lets the reels float free. When a jackpot is lined up, he pulls away the magnet and—presto! One of these cheats was spotted working a machine. The security guards gave chase, and as he ran down the street he suddenly came to a screeching halt. The magnet he was using was so large that he accidentally magnetized himself to a lamp post.

Wiring—Inserting a wire in the machine's coin return to manipulate the reels.

Shimming—Using a thin sheet of plastic to trigger the machine's free play escalator.

Spooning—Inserting a special tool into the coin drop to keep the pay slide in the open position.

Card sharks are also a big problem for the casinos, but by dealing the cards face up it's pretty hard to cheat at blackjack nowadays. Still, whenever you find a game where the player gets to touch his cards, you'll find the following:

Dauber—A card-marking substance (ultraviolet paint, etc.) is daubed on the back of certain cards, and soon the cheat knows what the dealer's hole card is.

Crimper—A skillful card handler can put a bend in a card so slight that only he can detect it. Sometimes a sloppy dealer can unwittingly bend the cards, too, and a sharp player doesn't have to go to the trouble of bending the cards himself.

Sander—With a small piece of sandpaper usually hidden by a band aid, the cheat will sand the edge of certain cards during the game. Since the sand work is so slight, this practice is hard for the dealer or supervisor to detect.

Presser—This player makes a motion with his hand that he doesn't want another card. While doing so, he drops another chip on top of his bet.

Mucker—By sleight of hand, he takes cards out of the game, hides them in a specially-designed holder, then brings them back into play later.

Glimmer—This character uses a tiny concealed mirror to get a reflection of the dealer's hole card.

Beware, too, of blackjack players using hidden computers. One group won a quarter of a million dollars in six weeks time before they were apprehended in Atlantic City.

At the dice tables, surveillance is on the lookout for shooters who try to slide the dice down the table without rolling them, or for someone sneaking loaded dice into the game. One of the casino's precautions against loaded dice is the use of balancing calipers, and all dice at the game will be checked with this tool before use. At baccarat and blackjack, there's the constant fear of somebody bringing a "cooler" into the game (a shoe of cards prearranged in a particular sequence). At keno and in sports books, there will always be someone trying to cash counterfeit tickets.

Another method employed by cheats is stealing the casino's roulette ball and replacing it with another ball with a metal insert inside. The cheater then attempts to control the ball's movement by means of a large magnet he conceals near the wheel. One cheat had his magnet hidden inside a fake plaster cast on his arm. Unfortunately, the magnet was stronger than the cheat anticipated, and the ball leapt off the wheel altogether and stuck to his cast!

Another problem at any table game is past-posting, where a player makes a bet or increases his bet after a winning decision has occurred. When caught, one of these players can always feign ignorance, which makes criminal intent difficult to ascertain. There are also a select few who earn a living by making claim bets. They'll go to a busy table, then try to get paid for a bet they didn't make. In many instances, the casinos will pay them just to get the game going again.

Here's another true story, this one concerning former First Lady Eleanor Roosevelt. In 1948, she was in Las Vegas on her way to visit Hoover Dam, and made a stop at the old El Rancho Vegas on the Strip. The casino owner invited her to play a 25¢ slot machine, but she had no luck whatsoever. The owner grabbed his slot mechanic and had him fix another machine so it would pay off eight out of ten times. "You're playing a cold machine, Mrs. Roosevelt," he told her. "Why don't you try this one?"

Soon the quarters were dropping into her tray and she was chortling with delight. She wound up cashing in $680, and never did visit Hoover Dam. She went to her death never once suspecting that she had been "took" in Las Vegas.

What will the casino do with a suspected cheater?

He will be detained by casino security. The Gaming Control Board will be notified, as well as local police. He will then be arrested and charged with a felony. If found guilty of cheating the casino, he could be fined and/or imprisoned. At the very least, his mug shot will be distributed to all other Nevada casinos, and he'll be barred from all state gaming establishments.

In one casino where the cards were dealt face down, the dealer got a blackjack. One of the players scooped up his bet and walked hurriedly away from the table. The dealer notified her supervisor, who had a security guard grab the player before he got out the door. Meanwhile, the dealer turned over the player's cards. He had a blackjack, too!

How many cheaters are nabbed in Nevada casinos each year?

According to the International Casino Surveillance Network of Sparks, Nevada, there were 468 cheaters apprehended in Nevada casinos for the last year records were available. Fifty-nine percent were patrons, and the others were gaming employees. Twenty-one arrests were made at blackjack tables; 145 at slot machines. Men cheaters outnumbered women two to one.

Are most cheaters professional gamblers?

Surprisingly, no. In fact, a recent survey shows that 95% of the people who cheat at private games are "friends" of the victims. Since it's illegal to ship gambling equipment across state lines, most of these snakes get their loaded dice and marked cards from magic stores! Of course, there's always a little blurb on the box that reads, "Not to be used for any unlawful purpose." Yeah, sure.

What is the single biggest enforcement problem facing the Gaming Control Board?

The illegal sale of slot machines out of state is the number one headache, according to a Gaming Board representative. "We have a number of cases pending now against licensed distributors that have been fudging their records by shipping these machines to illegal jurisdictions, such as Indian tribes in other states. This is a cardinal sin because they're deceiving the Gaming Commission, and this is a violation of the regulatory partnership that has historically worked so well in the state of Nevada."

What about dishonest dealers or supervisors?

It happens, but it's not as big a problem as you might think. After all, if an employee gets caught cheating, he loses his sheriff's card. Without that card, he'll never get another casino job. For some people, however, it's a risk worth taking. The problem is that if they get away with it once, they'll try it again—and eventually they're going to get caught.

Not only are casino employees under the watchful eye of surveillance cameras, but there are also "outside" surveillance agents, posing as players, who are constantly on the premises looking for anything out of the ordinary.

Outside surveillance agents once caught a dice dealer putting up bets for a confederate with the casino's money. Here's how this plan was hatched. The confederate gave the dealer enough money to place each number for $5. Instead, the dealer placed $25 of the casino's money on each number. Not only did the guilty dealer get fired as a result, but so did the boxman, the floor supervisor, and the other dealers on the crew.

In one casino, the boxman and the floor supervisor on a dice game teamed up on a swindle that went like this. The supervisor would ask to see the table card (which lists all markers taken during the shift). The boxman would slip a couple of $100 chips inside the card, then hand it to the supervisor. The supervisor would nonchalantly study the card, letting the chips drop into his hand—and eventually into his pocket.

Here's a baccarat scam that took place at three Nevada casinos in the mid-1990s. One of the players recorded the value of the cards on a scorecard during the game. Nothing wrong with that; everybody does it. But when the cards were re-shuffled at the end of the shoe, the dealer didn't mix in the batch of cards that was recorded by the player. This is called a "slug." When the game continued, the player looked for cards indicating the start of the slug and began to bet accordingly. This would tip off the other players at the table. By the time the group was apprehended, they had taken the casinos for $700,000.

The most sophisticated ruses these days are marker scams. A confederate gives the name of a known player to the supervisor and tells her he wants a marker for $10,000. The player gets the money, then signs the marker. The supervisor and dealer initial the table card, certifying that the player did in fact take a marker for $10,000. The player makes one bet, then leaves the table with the rest of the money. After the table is closed, the supervisor gets the $10,000 marker from the pit clerk. She pockets the check, signs off the marker, and forges the dealer's initials on the table card. Later, she gives the marker back to the player, and the player gives her half the money! Not bad for 20 minutes of skullduggery.

This scheme backfired in one casino because the dealer recognized the name of the known player, and knew that the man playing wasn't the same person. She reported this to the pit manager, who didn't take any action on the matter. The pit manager, who wasn't even in on the scam, lost her job as a result.

That's the problem with stealing. A thief always takes a few innocent people with him when he goes.

Why do the dealers wear aprons?

The aprons cover the dealers' pockets, thereby making it harder for somebody to "accidentally" drop a chip or two in the old Levis. For the same reason you'll never see dealers wearing shirts with French cuffs or cuffed pants.

A blackjack dealer was caught by a surveillance camera stuffing $25 chips into his pants. Taken to a back room, he was asked to empty his pockets, and out came almost $600 in chips. "Where did you get these?" he was asked.

Without a moment's hesitation the dealer replied, "These are my wife's pants! She was out gambling last night and must have forgot to take the money out of her pockets."

Why do the dealers insist that larger denomination chips be placed on the bottom when a bet is made?

It's to ensure that nobody adds a chip to their bet after they win. The thinking is that it's more difficult to sneak a larger chip on the bottom of a bet than on the top.

What should I do to protect myself in a casino?

The number one crime in Las Vegas is theft. When playing any machine or table game, always keep your purse in your lap (or ask the supervisor for a purse strap that hooks right to the table) and keep a close eye on shopping bags and anything else you own. In one casino, a physically-handicapped man was sitting at a blackjack table, and somebody stole his wheelchair!

Here's one of the newest scams. You're playing a dollar slot machine when a man stops at your side. "Excuse me," he says, "is that your dollar?" You look down and there's a dollar token on the floor next to your machine. You reach down to pick it up, and suddenly your purse and cup of coins are gone! The man dropped the dollar on the floor when you weren't looking, and a confederate was just waiting for you to take the bait.

Don't carry large sums of cash. Men should beware of pickpockets, who usually hang out in crowded areas. I know it isn't macho, but wear a fanny pack.

Another problem in casinos is the chip thief, or "rail bird." While your attention is diverted, this bum will sneak a couple of chips out of your rack—and by the time you realize it, he's already gone. When you arrange the chips in your rack, put the highest denomination chips in the center and surround them on either end with $1 chips. Chances are a thief will move on to an easier target.

Otherwise, here's what can happen. A middle-aged woman (over 30, under 90) spent every afternoon at the same dice table. She would lean forward to make a bet with her right hand. Meanwhile, her left hand went under her right arm and into the adjacent player's chip rack, retrieving a couple of chips which she would slip into her pocket. On the day she was finally caught, she had over $2,000 in her pocket.

Don't keep valuables in your room. Either use a floor safe (a third of the hotels in Vegas offer them), or get a safety deposit box at the front desk or cashier's cage. There's usually no charge for this service.

Why can't I keep my purse on the table when I'm playing blackjack?

You can't place any item on a blackjack table that's

larger than a playing card. This is why cocktails are served on small round coasters instead of regular napkins. After all, what's to keep some unscrupulous player from tucking one of his cards underneath a larger object, then retrieving it later. Keep your purse in your lap, or give it to your husband. That's what husbands are for.

Who else has a key to my safety deposit box?

Nobody. There's only one key for each safety deposit box, and you've got it. If you lose it, the box has to be drilled open in front of three witnesses, and it'll cost you at least $20 to replace it.

How much money is kept in the cashier's cage?

It varies according to hotel size and number of games, but for the average Strip casino the amount of cash on hand is anywhere from $250,000 to over $1 million.

How does the casino transport cash to the bank?

By armored truck—and no, they don't pick up hitch-hikers.

How does the casino guard against counterfeit chips?

Every casino has a complete inventory of the number of gaming chips on hand, including those on each table game and at the cashier's cage. These chips are counted every 24 hours. Usually the casino will be a few chips short, due to people taking some home as souvenirs. In the event there is an extremely large surplus of chips, the casino will check for possible counterfeits. It's a rare occurrence, however.

The only chip counterfeiting scheme I can remember firsthand was at the old Dunes Hotel, where an enterprising individual pasted fake $25 inserts on a batch of 25¢

chips from a Reno casino which were the same color. He may have gotten away with it forever, except for the fact that one of the inserts peeled off—exposing the real value of the chip underneath.

Has a casino ever refused to pay a slot machine jackpot?

Yes, but usually if the machine was tampered with or if it malfunctioned in some way. In the case of a machine malfunction, the casino's position (which has been accepted by the courts) is that a jackpot isn't really a jackpot if the technology is faulty.

Here's what happened in March of 1997 at the Nevada Palace in Las Vegas. A Tacoma, Washington, man was playing a quarter slot machine when it jammed. He wanted to keep playing the same machine so he waited while a slot technician opened it and reattached a loose wire. With the door of the machine open, the technician spun the reels to make sure the machine was working properly. Voila! The reels lined up on a $1.4 million jackpot.

The player figured it was his jackpot because he had been playing the machine, and went before the Gaming Control Board claiming punitive damages for his "mental anguish." His claim was rejected, and now he probably owes his lawyer another $1.4 million.

On the other hand, voicing one's displeasure with a malfunctioning machine can sometimes reap substantial rewards. In one Las Vegas casino, a high roller was playing a $5 slot machine, dumping in $15 each spin. Suddenly two winning symbols lined up. The third winning symbol clicked into place, then backed up just a fraction. It was enough, however, to negate a payoff of $180,000.

The high roller screamed bloody murder. The casino, which didn't want to lose the high roller's business, offered to split the difference—and gave the high roller a check for $90,000.

BAD LUCK

A young man from Arkansas won $1,061,811 on a slot machine at Caesars Palace. The problem was that the young man was only 19 years old. The Gaming Control Board ruled that since Nevada law prohibits anyone under the age of 21 from gambling, the man was not entitled to the money.

GOOD LUCK

A woman spotted two free plays that someone inadvertently left on a quarter slot machine. She pushed the "play" button, and lined up three stars. Her prize? A brand new Ford Mustang convertible! She won a $29,000 car for the lowly investment of 50¢, and it wasn't even her 50¢ to begin with.

BAD LUCK

On January 26, 2000, a Las Vegas cocktail waitress won $34 million on a Megabucks slot machine. She split the winnings with her boyfriend, quit her job, and got married. On March 11, 2000, her car was rear-ended by a drunk driver. Her sister was killed, and she was paralyzed. It all happened within two month's time.

GOOD LUCK

A woman won $1,200 on a quarter slot machine. While she was waiting to be paid, she began playing a dollar slot machine—and won another $1.1 million! It all happened within one hour's time.

A Mississippi woman lined up a royal flush on a video slot machine in this order: ace, king, queen, jack, 10. A sequential royal paid a whopping $250,000 in the casino where she was playing, so she was quite happy to say the least. That is, until she was told the sequential royal had to line up in the *opposite* direction: 10, jack, queen, king, ace. A Mississippi hearing officer ruled the language on the machine was unclear, and she got the money.

At the Venetian in Las Vegas, a woman lined up three double diamond symbols on a $1 slot. The payout display indicated that she won the machine's progressive jackpot, which was a whopping $175,215. Sorry, the Venetian said, the machine had been fitted with the wrong payout glass and wasn't linked to the progressive jackpot. The jackpot was only worth $1,600. She appealed to the Nevada Gaming Control Board. "Hey, it said I won. I want my money!" In a 3-0 ruling, the control board awarded her the whole $175,000. "It is important for customers to trust Nevada casinos," the board said. "Customers need to be sure that if they win, they'll be paid. It's one of the things that sets Nevada apart."

At Harrah's Ak-Chin casino in Arizona, a former migrant worker lined up the winning symbols on a $300,000 jackpot. When officials from the slot company told her the machine had malfunctioned, she hired a lawyer and contacted the news media. The ensuing barrage of news coverage resulted in such bad press for Harrah's that they paid her anyway.

Don't count on this happening to you, though. International Gaming Technology, which commands 70% of slot machine revenues in North America, refuses to pay such claims. "If we did," an IGT spokesperson said, "we'd be opening ourselves to a blackmail situation from people making false claims."

What are some of the reasons why casinos get sued?

A lawyer in the legal department of one Vegas casino says that most lawsuits are over personal injuries. If you get hurt on casino property, the legal department will investigate your claim, and talk to all eyewitnesses. Sometimes the casino will settle with you out of court, but

don't count on it. Otherwise, the casino will get a reputa-
tion as an easy mark.

One person actually sued the casino where he was
staying because the shower drain overflowed, thereby
"exposing him to the AIDS virus." In another case, a
woman claimed carpal tunnel syndrome after a folding
closet door fell on top of her. She lost, too.

A case still under litigation in Mississippi concerns a
gambler with a sticky situation. He says he got stuck to a
toilet seat that someone smeared with glue and had to
waddle across the casino floor with the seat still attached
to seek help. Not so, said the Silver Star Casino, and
they're fighting the man's claim for $50,000.

A California woman sued a Vegas casino, claiming
someone else hit a jackpot on "her" machine while she was
having dinner. She'd been playing the same machine for
12 hours, and alleged that a slot worker offered to shut
the machine down while she got something to eat.
Unfortunately, she was gone for an hour and 45 minutes.
By the time she returned, the machine had been turned
back on and somebody else had hit it for $100,000!
Sorry, said the casino. Saving a machine for a gambler is
a matter of individual casino policy and is not covered
under state gaming regulations.

Can injured employees sue the casino?

Usually not. Like every other state, Nevada has a no-
fault insurance system, which means that if a worker is
injured on premises, nobody is held responsible. Disability
payments and settlements to injured workers are either
paid by self-insured casinos or by the Employers Insurance
Company of Nevada. Over 125,000 claims are handled in
Nevada each year, and recent statistics show that 1 in
every 6 Nevada workers gets hurt on the job. How? Here
are a couple I culled from a stack of accident reports. A
restroom porter hurt his neck carrying towels; a maid got

something in her eye while vacuuming a room; and a show-room captain sprained his wrist opening a bottle of wine. Does anybody want to give to their collections?

If my wife hit a slot machine jackpot for $250,000 and died a week later, what would I get?

Life.

Why do most hotels use cards now instead of keys for room entry?

I never liked those little cards until I learned more about them. First, they have no room number printed on them, so if you lose your card nobody will know which door it fits. Secondly, every time you unlock your door with this card, it activates a centralized computer. Now the hotel has a record of each exact moment when your door was unlocked, and who opened it. (See computer readout.)

Are gambling losses legally collectible?

Yes, and they have been since 1983. A marker is technically a personal check. The casino will usually give you 30 days to pay it. If you don't, you'll be contacted by telephone and asked to either pay it in full or make monthly payments. In rare instances, the casino will settle with you at a discounted rate, but you'll never be allowed to play on credit again.

A California doctor ran up a $3,000 marker on one of his Vegas trips. Thinking that he was under no legal obligation to pay a gambling debt, he wrote a hot check for the marker, then threatened legal action if the casino didn't stop bothering him. Here came an arrest warrant from the state of Nevada. Writing a hot check to pay a gambling debt is in violation of Nevada regulation NRS 205.130, and is a felony in the state of Nevada. The doctor sent a $3,000 money order to the casino the following day.

```
Filtered Report generated Thu 01/26/99 10:37:53 by MARLOK DEPT.

Filter 5 ROOM ACTIVITY
From: Sun 04/05/99 00:00:00
To:   Fri 04/10/99 23:59:59

Keys:        ALL KEYS
Doors:       NONE
Rooms:       16068
Operators:   ALL OPERATORS

Sun 04/05/99 01:37:08 Room 16068 unlocked for guest key 2C7E5A
Sun 04-04/99 01:37:22 Room 16068 unlocked for guest key 2C7E5A
Insert next floppy for A:\920405.DAT

Sun 04/05/99 03:37:28 Room 16068 unlocked for guest key 2C7E5A
Sun 04/05/99 11:38:11 Room 16068 invalid entry attempt key 9EAD12
Sun 04/05/99 11:38:11 Room 16968 unlocked for maid key 786309
Sun 04/05/99 12:12:48 Con 10 Op F.D.LOG 7 Room 16068 Guest 2D53A2 Replace guest
Sun 04/05/99 12:12:56 Con 10 Op F.D.LOG 7 Room 16068 Guest 2E0ACF Assign guest
Sun 04/05/99 13:13:14 Room 16068 invalid entry attempt key 2D532D
Sun 04/05/99 13:13:33 Room 16068 invalid entry attempt key 2D532D
Sun 04/05/99 13:13:33 Room 16068 invalid entry attempt key 2D532D
Sun 04/05/99 13:13:33 Room 16068 invalid entry attempt key 2D532D
Sun 04/05/99 13:13:33 Room 16068 invalid entry attempt key 2D532D
Sun 04/05/99 13:13:51 Room 16068 unlocked for guest key 2E0ACF
Insert next floppy for A:\920405.DAT

Sun 04/05/99 18:42:35 Room 16068 unlocked for guest key 2D532D
Sun 04/05/99 18:42:35 Room 16068 unlocked for guest key 2D532D
Sun 04/05/99 18:42:49 Room 16068 unlocked for guest key 2D532D
Sun 04/05/99 21:02:46 Room 16068 unlocked for guest key 2D532D
Sun 04/05/99 21:05:55 Room 16068 unlocked for guest key 2D532D
Sun 04/05/99 21:06:09 Room 16068 unlocked for guest key 2D532D
Sun 04/05/99 21:06:23 Room 16068 unlocked for guest key 2D532D
Sun 04/05/99 21:06:23 Room 16068 unlocked for guest key 2D532D
Sun 04/05/99 21:06:37 Room 16068 unlocked for guest key 2D532D
Sun 04/05/99 21:06:51 Room 16068 unlocked for guest key 2D532D
Sun 04/05/99 21:06:51 Room 16068 unlocked for guest key 2D532D
Sun 04/05/99 21:07:06 Room 16068 unlocked for guest key 2D532D
Sun 04/05/99 21:07:21 Room 16068 unlocked for guest key 2D532D
Sun 04/05/99 21:07:34 Room 16068 unlocked for guest key 2D532D
Sun 04/05/99 21:07:34 Room 16068 unlocked for guest key 2D532D
Sun 04/05/99 21:07:48 Room 16068 unlocked for guest key 2D532D
Sun 04/05/99 21:08:02 Room 16068 unlocked for guest key 2D532D
Sun 04/05/99 23:53:35 Room 16068 unlocked for guest key 2D532D
Sun 04/06/99 00:50:12 Room 16068 unlocked for guest key 2D532D
Sun 04/06/99 01:28:08 Room 16068 unlocked for guest key 2D532D
Sun 04/06/99 09:42:07 Room 16068 unlocked for guest key 2D532D
Sun 04/06/99 10:37:49 Room 16068 unlocked for guest key 2D532D
```

How many bad checks are written in Las Vegas each year?

For the last year that such records were available, the total number of hot checks (including three to my lawyer) was 20,788.

Why will I be asked for my name if I make a large bet in the casino?

For one thing, the casino wants to know who you are in case you win big. If you do win, don't be surprised if you're offered a sumptuous meal in the gourmet restaurant or maybe even a free room for the night. The casino wants a chance to get that money back.

The supervisor will also want to rate your play, in case you request any complimentaries later. Since you've given him your name, he knows who you are, and it makes getting a comp that much easier.

When will I be asked for identification?

You'll be asked for identification if you set up a line of credit or make a cash deposit at the casino cage; if you hit a taxable jackpot at keno, bingo, or a slot machine; if you cash a check; if you cash out over $10,000 in chips; or if you wager over $10,000 in cash in a 24-hour period. The last two are in compliance with Federal Regulation 6A (similar to Title 31 of the U.S. Treasury's Bank Secrecy Act), which requires that all cash transactions of over $10,000 be reported to the Treasury Department. The reason behind this regulation, according to the government, is to discourage money laundering; i.e., changing small bills into big bills. You'll run into the same regulation at banks. There's a moral here somewhere, and I think it's to change your small bills into big bills through a loan shark or illegal bookie before you come to Las Vegas.

Can I cash a personal check in the casino?

Yes, as long as you have a major credit card and a driver's license or other valid form of photo ID. Most casinos have a cash limit of anywhere from $200 up to $1,000. For larger amounts, the casino will usually have to call your bank during business hours.

Is prostitution legal in Nevada?

It's legal in some counties, but not in Clark County (Las Vegas) or Washoe County (Reno). That doesn't mean there aren't any hookers in Vegas. Over 2,500 are arrested each year. Due to the threat of AIDS, however, I would advise steering clear of them.

By the way, here's a true story told to me by a casino cashier. A young prostitute approached the casino cage with $500 in Japanese yen. "Could I get this changed into American money?" she asked the cashier.

"Certainly," the cashier replied, counting out the American equivalent of $4.20. Somebody got the last laugh that night, and it wasn't the prostitute.

Is kleptomania catching?

No, it's *taking*.

What is the only city in Nevada where gambling is against the law?

Gambling is illegal in Boulder City, 25 miles south of Las Vegas and the site of Hoover Dam. Hard liquor was also banned there until 1969. The reason for banning booze and gambling was to keep up worker productivity while the dam was being built.

How do I interest a casino in a new game I've invented?

You have to submit the game to the Nevada Gaming Control Board, where engineers and technicians will test it for a period of up to four months. Factors taken into consideration include the game's randomness, payback percentage, and overall security features. Then the game will be field-tested, after which it will either be approved or denied by the Control Board. Expenses for all these tests are borne by the game's inventor. Then you'll have to sell a casino on the idea of replacing another game with your game because casino space is at a premium.

Your best bet would be to sell a gaming company or gaming consultant an interest in your game, and then let them take care of all these factors. Look under "Gaming" in the Las Vegas yellow pages.   Or plan on attending a gaming exposition in Las Vegas, and sell your game in person. Call the Las Vegas Convention and Visitor's Authority for a calendar of gaming expos.

What if I am attacked by a casino mascot, such as the MGM lion or one of the white tigers at the Mirage?

Do everything in the following order of importance:

1) Get the names and addresses of all eyewitnesses

2) Call your lawyer

3) Call the casino's lawyer

4) Contact the Nevada Attorney General's office

5) Notify the news media

6) Pack the severed limb in ice

7) Go to the hospital

10
Statisticzzzz

How fast is Las Vegas growing?

According to statistics, between 4,000 and 6,000 people move to Las Vegas every month. However, as soon as their mug shots show up on *America's Most Wanted*, the majority of them leave again.

In job growth rate, Vegas is usually in the top ten, with 43,000 new jobs on average each year.

What is the average price of a new home in Las Vegas?

About 20,000 new homes are built in Clark County each year, with a median price of around $150,000. This price includes everything but a decent-sized back yard. So if you want a pool or a nice tree, you'll have to go in partners with your next-door neighbor.

How much of the parking on the Strip is used by tourists, and how much is used by employees?

Believe it or not, 60% of the parking at Strip casinos is by employees. Authorities say it's the tail fins on the employees' 1965 Cadillacs that take up all the room.

What is the percentage of people who use cab service in Las Vegas?

Roughly one out of every four tourists in Las Vegas use taxis. That doesn't sound too bad, until you figure that if there are 60,000 tourists in town, then 15,000 of them are trying to get a cab somewhere.

How many cabs are there in Las Vegas?

As this goes to press, there are 965 cabs in the city, and the turn-light indicators work on 40 of them.

What is the percentage of visitors who stay in hotels while in Las Vegas?

Roughly 92% stay in hotels or motels. (The other 8% stay at our house.)

How hot does it get in Las Vegas?

It's not uncommon to see the temperature get up to 110 degrees during the last two weeks of July, which is the hottest time of the year in Las Vegas. It's even worse in nearby Laughlin, which recorded the state's record high temperature in 1994—a blistering 125 degrees. Of course, with the wind chill factor it was really only 119.

Average highs and lows:

Jan–Mar	63°	39°
Apr–June	89°	60°
July–Sept	101°	72°
Oct–Dec	71°	44°

How many days of sunshine does Las Vegas get each year?

According to the weather bureau, the sun shines in Vegas about 294 days per year (211 clear days, 83 partly cloudy). The humidity hovers around 29%, and the average temperature is 66.3 degrees.

How much rain does Las Vegas get?

An average of 4.8 inches a year. Unfortunately, it's usually all on the same day.

Does it ever snow in Las Vegas?

Hardly ever. In fact, there's only been one big snowfall that I can remember, and that was over 20 years ago. On that occasion, I think it snowed eight inches. (Well, the men claimed it was eight inches; the women said it was more like five inches.)

What is the percentage of young people who visit Las Vegas?

Only 11% of Vegas visitors are under the age of 21. At Circus Circus, which is probably the most kid-oriented casino in Vegas, two of every three visitors are over 40.

What is the percentage of international visitors?

At last report, 13% of the people who visit Las Vegas are from foreign countries such as Canada, Mexico, and Mississippi.

How many people come to Las Vegas each year for conventions?

Around 4 million people a year fly to Vegas for conventions annually, and roughly 9,000 of them actually go to the convention seminars.

What is the most popular form of transportation for people traveling to Las Vegas?

Fifty-two percent arrive in Las Vegas by car, and 48% by air. For people *leaving* Las Vegas, 38% take the bus and 62% hitchhike.

How many people pass through McCarran International Airport each day?

The average is over 52,000 a day. This is expected to hit 150,000 per day by the end of the decade (or 55 million passengers a year), at which time the airport will be maxed out. Here's another interesting statistic. McCarran can handle 85 flights an hour if all conditions are perfect.

How many days does the average tourist stay in Las Vegas?

According to the Las Vegas Convention & Visitors Authority, the average stay per visit is four days and three nights.

How many people go to shows while they're in Las Vegas?

Almost half (46%) see some kind of show, and 78% of those would rather see a big production show than anything else. Also up in popularity are lounge shows, with 32% attendance by Vegas visitors. On the other hand, big name entertainment and comedy revues have fallen in popularity over the last few years.

How much time does the average tourist spend gambling?

Roughly four hours a day.

Do people gamble more during the week or on weekends?

According to a survey by Terry Nosek of *The Source*, weekday guests in Las Vegas gamble 26% more per day than weekend visitors.

What is the average bet at a table game?

About $13 a hand.

What denomination slot machine does the average visitor prefer?

Sixty-four percent play quarter slots, 21% play nickels, and only 14% play $1 slots.

How many slot players play the maximum number of coins per hand?

Surprisingly, only three people in ten play properly by inserting the maximum number of coins.

What is the average tourist's gambling budget?

A little over $500 per visit, with another $400 for accommodations, entertainment, meals, drinks, transportation, and shopping.

What is the average tourist's favorite game?

Reel slot machines are far and away the most popular game of chance, favored by 52% of all gamblers. Seventeen percent play video poker, 16% play blackjack, 6% play craps, and a total of 9% play other games in the casino.

How much money does the average tourist lose while gambling?

According to the Nevada Gaming Control Board, a total of $156.75 per tourist goes toward the casino's next high rise.

How many slot machines are there in Las Vegas?

There are 120,776 slot machines, or one for every nine Las Vegas residents.

What is the total number of slot machines in Nevada?

At last report, there were 173,716 one-armed bandits in the state.

Which casino in Las Vegas has the greatest number of slot machines?

The MGM Grand has a total of 3,720 slot machines. This compares with only 20 slots at the Loose Caboose Saloon. (I knew I'd get the name "Loose Caboose" in here somewhere.)

What is the most popular denomination of machine in Las Vegas?

There are 68,799 quarter slot machines, compared with only 156 penny slots and around 23,000 nickel slots and dollar slots.

How many blackjack tables are there in Las Vegas?

A grand total of 2,336, or more than all other table games combined.

What are the least popular games in the casino?

Sic Bo (only three games statewide), Over/Under 13 (one game), and Red Dog (two games).

How many gambling chips does the average casino use?

There are approximately 771,700 chips just at the MGM Grand Casino. If they were stacked one on top of the other, they would make a pile over 1.5 miles high!

How much are all the chips in a casino worth?

Between $50 and $100 million, but remember they're not all in use at any given time. In fact, most major casinos keep special chips in their vaults that can be worth as much as $100,000 apiece. These are for special players whose betting limits can be as high as $250,000 a hand. Personally, I like the $100,000 chips. They have a nice feel to them because they're not used as often, and they make wonderful little key chains.

What is the highest denomination chip?

The London Club at the Aladdin in Las Vegas has a $10 million chip, which is actually a black and white plastic plaque measuring four by seven inches. The chip is probably more for bragging rights than actual use. Can you imagine walking up to a dice game and tossing a $10 million chip on the table? "Give me nine $1 million chips, nine $100,000 chips, nine hundred and ninety-nine $100 chips, and the rest in dollars, please."

How many dice does the average casino use in a year's time?

About 5,000 sets of dice a year—which costs the casino over $12,000! (Then they sell them in the gift shop for $24,000.)

How many decks of cards are being shuffled in the casino at any given moment?

The MGM Grand, which is the biggest in Vegas, has more than 800 decks of cards being shuffled at any given time.

How many decks of cards does the average casino use in a year's time?

Around 300,000 decks. The Aladdin in Las Vegas came up with this interesting statistic. If you placed each playing card end to end, they would stretch more than

852 miles—or about the distance from Las Vegas to Cheyenne, Wyoming.

How much does it cost to carpet a casino?

One Strip resort spent $2 million on new carpeting, and due to foot traffic had to replace it after only six years! That brings up another interesting question. What does a casino do with its old carpet? Why, it sells it to a smaller casino.

How much food and booze does a casino go through in a year's time?

According to statistics, over 100 million meals are served each year in Las Vegas. The buffet at Circus Circus serves more people every day—about 10,000—than any other restaurant in the world. The MGM Grand serves 30,000 meals a day (or almost 11 million meals a year), so you can imagine what their grocery bill is. In a year's time, the MGM uses 18 million eggs, 292,000 pounds of coffee, and 4.4 million doughnuts just for breakfast!

The most complete breakdown on annual usage comes from Caesars Palace: 11.7 million Kleenex tissues; 249,600 rolls of toilet paper; 240 million gallons of water; 100,000 pens; 12,000 ashtrays; 400,000 cocktail and dinner napkins; 187,000 eight-ounce glasses; 600,000 drinking glass bags; 74,880 heads of lettuce; 2.8 million eggs; 93,600 cucumbers; 200,200 pounds of pork loin; 26,400 pounds of tenderloin; 2.1 million ounces of tomato juice; 1.1 million ounces of orange juice; 2 million maraschino cherries; 1.3 million ounces of ketchup; 2.5 million pats of butter; 156,000 pounds of coffee; 520,000 glasses of milk; 744,000 bottles of beer; and 594,000 shots of vodka.

(Thanks to Debbie Munch of Caesars for what she calls these "gee whiz" statistics.)

What is the tallest hotel in Las Vegas?

New York-New York, on the Vegas Strip, is the tallest building in the state at 47 stories. It's dwarfed in size, though, by the Stratosphere tower. At 112 stories, it's the tallest free-standing observatory in the United States.

Has anyone jumped off the Brooklyn Bridge at New York-New York?

Not yet, but give 'em time, give 'em time.

Which Las Vegas casino has the biggest sign?

The $9 million marquee at the Las Vegas Hilton is the biggest free-standing sign in the world. It's almost 30 stories high (279 feet), 164 feet wide, and has 77,000 light bulbs—enough to light over 600 homes.

How many light bulbs are there on the Las Vegas Strip?

Nobody knows how many lights are on the Strip, but according to Nevada Power Company the annual demand for electricity would power 86,000 homes. Meanwhile, the annual demand for electricity in downtown Las Vegas would power another 17,000 homes. To give you a rough idea on the number of lights in Las Vegas, there are 2,100,000 bulbs in the Fremont Street Experience alone!

Viewed from space, Las Vegas is the brightest spot on the planet. (Source: Nevada Power Company)

What is the annual power bill for an average Las Vegas casino?

Three million dollars—so always turn the lights off in the casino when you leave.

How much dirty laundry do the hotels in Vegas go through each week?

Mission Industries, the largest cleaning plant in Las Vegas, washes over 4 million pounds of dirty sheets, towels, and uniforms every week! Here are more amazing facts. The MGM Grand, which has its own cleaning plant, uses 22 miles of fresh sheets every day, along with 12,000 bath towels, 18,000 wash cloths, and 15,000 pillowcases. The Bellagio goes through 44,000 pounds of linen daily, including 10,000 king-size sheets and pillowcases, 7,500 bath towels, 9,000 wash cloths, and 4,000 bath rugs.

How many items are hocked in Las Vegas pawn shops each month?

Approximately 20,000 pawn tickets are written every month in Las Vegas hock shops on such items as hand guns, silencers, rifles, Uzi automatic weapons, switchblade knives, stilettos, handcuffs, brass knuckles, and all the other delightful relics of the 20th century.

11
Getting Around

How should I dress in a casino?

The days of evening gowns and dinner jackets are long past. Today it's whatever makes you feel good (although shirts and shoes are still required in some of the fancier joints). If you plan on dining in a fancy restaurant, bring a jacket and tie. Otherwise, wear jeans or other informal wear, and comfortable walking shoes. Or dress as my mother-in-law does: slinky muu muu, lighted tennis shoes, and Carmen Miranda headpiece with artificial bananas and pineapples. After all, this is Vegas, where anything goes—and usually does.

What else should my wife and I pack for our trip to Las Vegas?

First, check the weather forecast. In the summer, you'll want lighter clothing, and of course heavier attire for winter wear. Unfortunately, the weather can change from day to day, so plan on bringing the following:

WOMEN: Loose-fitting beige coat, scarf, tailored suit, walking pumps, sandals, dinner jacket, casual jacket, non-sheer tailored blouses (3), slipover sweaters (2), shorts (3), tennis shoes, jeans, navy skirt, black skirt, brown skirt, cotton shirts (5), undies, costume jewelry, dinner dress, cocktail dress, house dress, lounging pajamas, robe, slippers, bathing suit, cap with visor, sunglasses, sun-screen, lipstick, mascara, eye shadow, rouge, pocket-sized magnifying makeup mirror, toiletries.

MEN: Tank tops (2), cutoffs (1), thongs, toothbrush.

Should I bring my expensive jewelry?

If you've got it, flaunt it! Too much jewelry in Las Vegas is just enough. Remember, though, that when you're not wearing it, leave it in a casino safety deposit box.

Are children allowed in the casino?

Only if they're working there as assistant vice-presidents in charge of casino operations. Otherwise, children are allowed to walk through the casino, but they're prohibited from loitering near any gambling device or game of chance. Your best bet is to park the kids in the casino video arcade (with adult supervision) while you try your luck at the tables. For toddlers, there are baby-sitting services available at most casinos, and some even have interactive child care centers.

Caesars Palace roulette dealer Mike Brunsvold asked a young player for her driver's license, since she appeared to be under 21. The young lady handed Mike her license. Sure enough, she was 21 years old. "Look on the other side," she announced smugly. "You'll see that I'm an organ donor."

"Sorry," Mike replied. "I'm only allowed to take cash."

Is there a curfew for minors?

In Las Vegas, there's a 9 p.m. curfew for children under the age of 18.

I've heard that the Bellagio refuses admission to anyone under the age of 18 who is not a guest in the hotel. What am I supposed to do with my kids?

Bellagio's actual policy bans minors and children unless they are hotel guests or with someone who is attending a show, eating in a restaurant, or visiting the art gallery. You're better off sending them to the Hard Rock, where people *over* the age of 18 are not allowed.

Are there no-smoking sections in the casinos?

Silver City on the Las Vegas Strip was the only smoke-free establishment in town, and it went bankrupt. Most of the other casinos have no-smoking tables. Look for the signs. The day will probably never come when smoking is completely banned in Nevada casinos. If it does, Las Vegas will probably go up in smoke.

If you don't believe that, read the following statistics. Smokers make up 33% of the people who gamble. If they were forced to take ten-minute smoke breaks outdoors every hour, it would reduce their gambling time by 16%, resulting in a 5-year loss to the Nevada economy of $3.5 billion, plus 26,000 to 50,000 casino-related jobs.

While we're on the subject, here's a true story that happened in one fancy Las Vegas casino. A well-known publisher was betting $3,000 a hand at blackjack, and over a period of three days lost a whopping $2.3 million. (Well, when you're running bad, you're running bad.) After he left the table, the dealer filed a complaint that the publisher "deliberately" blew cigar smoke in her face.

If I lost $2.3 million, I think I'd be blowing smoke, too, only mine would be coming out of my ears!

What are some of the other attractions worth seeing in Las Vegas?

If you've got time, there's plenty to see outside the casinos, and I recommend visiting at least one of the following:

Mount Charleston, 35 miles northwest of Las Vegas, offers winter skiing, picnicking, hiking, and a couple of decent restaurants. It's also where Elvis snowmobiled in the movie *Viva Las Vegas*.

Red Rock Canyon features some of the most awesome red rock formations you'll ever see, with a 13-mile scenic loop winding through the park. Look for Ice Box Canyon, which Elvis climbed in *Viva Las Vegas*.

Valley of Fire State Park, 55 miles northeast of Vegas, has red rock formations, too, only these are shaped like animals and other objects. There are also some ancient petroglyphs and a neat trail that leads to Mouse's Tank, where Elvis bushwhacked a band of outlaws in *Viva Las Vegas*.

Lake Mead National Recreational Area, 25 miles south of Vegas, has more than 550 miles of shoreline, swimming, camping, boating, fishing, and my favorite sport—throwing popcorn to the carp. This is the largest man-made lake in the U.S., and it's where Elvis water-skied in *Viva Las Vegas*.

Hoover Dam, 34 miles south of Vegas, is one of the modern wonders of the world, with daily tours that have attracted more than 32 million visitors since it opened. That's almost as many people who saw the movie *Viva Las Vegas*.

A friend of mine from back home works in a casino. How can I find him in Las Vegas?

If you know where he works, call the casino's personnel office or scheduling department and find out what his hours are. They won't give you his home telephone number unless it's a family emergency.

What holidays are celebrated in Nevada?

New Year's, Labor Day, Memorial Day, Independence Day, Thanksgiving, Christmas, Bugsy Siegel's birthday, Al Capone's birthday, Lucky Luciano's birthday, and Halloween. I'm serious about Halloween. It's the same day that Nevada attained statehood in 1864.

What is the biggest holiday in Las Vegas?

It used to be New Year's, but believe it or not the biggest holiday in Vegas today isn't really a holiday. It's Super Bowl weekend! Anywhere from $50 to $70 million will be bet on the game statewide, and another $100 million will be spent on beer.

What are the most common complaints about Las Vegas?

Here they are in order:

1) "This room sucks."

2) "I've never seen such rude people in my life."

3) "Sevenenteen dollars for a tuna salad?"

4) "Is that the line waiting to get in the showroom, or is this a fire drill?"

5) "Hey, I'm getting the hang of this game. I'm only down $350."

I broke my glasses in the casino. Do I have to be examined all over?

No, just your eyes.

Where's the best place to people watch?

A survey taken by the readers of the *Las Vegas Review-Journal* picked the Fremont Street Experience downtown, while the newspaper itself selected the Forum

Shops at Caesars Palace. Personally, I like to stand on the side of the Strip near the entrance to the Mirage. You've probably seen me there. I'm the one selling copies of my books out of an old shopping cart.

Can I take pictures in the casino?

You can take pictures in non-gaming areas of the casino. In fact, most casinos encourage photo shoots in these sections. Great locales for camera buffs are:

- Top floor of the Horseshoe, Bally's, Flamingo Hilton, MGM Grand
- Voodoo Lounge at the Rio
- On the gondolas at the Venetian
- Downtown Las Vegas (the most photographed four blocks in the world)
- The statue of David in the Appian Way at Caesars Palace
- Any casino marquee
- The pyramid and Sphinx at the Luxor
- The big city skyline at New York-New York

If all else fails, do like everyone else does and buy a handful of picture post cards.

How can I get a cab without standing in line?

If there's a long line waiting for cabs outside the hotel entrance, backtrack through the casino to the side entrance. There are usually cabs there, too, and the lines are much shorter. The worst time to get a cab is right after the show breaks in the casino or while a convention is in town. During busy times, ask the doorman about shuttles or bus service. He has all that information, and will be glad to help you.

In Las Vegas, it's illegal for a taxi to pull over and pick

up a fare on the street. He can only pick up a fare on private property.

What are some of the unethical things cab drivers do to increase their fare?

Most cab drivers are honest, but there are a few who give the other two a bad name. The most common method of hiking the fare is by taking the long way to a fare's destination. (That's why you should always give explicit directions as to where you want to go.) Another ploy by some cab drivers is leaving the meter running after dropping off a fare. Then you hop in, and suddenly you already owe the driver $4. Remember, too, that the amount on the meter is the total fare, and not the fare for each person.

Exception: Fares leaving McCarran International Airport to the city are charged an additional $1.20 departure fee per cab. When you take a cab to the airport, this departure fee should not be charged. If an unscrupulous cab driver tries to charge you for this fee when you're leaving Las Vegas (and that's a common complaint), get his name and cab number and report him to the Taxicab Authority. The only thing you'll have to figure out is whether "Haseem" is his first name or his last name.

How much does the average Las Vegas cab driver make each year?

Around $38,000—less traffic fines of around $26,000 for such violations as tailgating, speeding, reckless driving, running red lights, parking in a fire zone, failure to yield right of way, ignoring emergency vehicles, leaving the scene of an accident, driving on the sidewalk, passing on the wrong side, using obscene language, littering, driving with their high beams on, and generally for just being rude and inconsiderate to every other driver on the face of the planet.

I want to valet park my car, but the valet lot is full. What do I do?

Give the valet attendant a $10 bill. He'll find a place to park your car, even if it's in his own garage. This works nine out of ten times.

Can I rent a limousine?

Yes, there are five licensed limousine services in Las Vegas, with prices ranging from $33–$45 an hour for a basic limo to $60–$80 an hour for a str-r-r-e-tch job. If you can't find a cab at the airport, take a limo to your hotel. It won't cost much more than a regular taxi, and you might find a $100 bill on the floor.

I can't get reservations for Danny Gans at the Mirage. What should I do?

Danny Gans is one of the most popular performers in Las Vegas, and it's almost impossible to get reservations. If you really want to see his show, stay at the Mirage on your next visit, or at another MGM property (Golden Nugget, Treasure Island, Bellagio, MGM Grand). Guests can make reservations up to three days in advance. Non-hotel patrons have to buy their tickets in person. If you still can't get tickets, call Danny at home on his private unlisted telephone number: 702-555-1282.

How do I keep from standing in line at a hotel buffet or coffee shop?

Scotch-tape a $20 bill to your forehead and ask the hostess for a table. Or ask a floor supervisor for a line pass. It doesn't cost the casino anything. If the supervisor asks you where you've been playing, tell him the truth. "I haven't played yet because I'm so hungry. But as soon as I get something to eat, I'll be right back." Other suggestions:

If you're handicapped, go directly to the cashier and you'll be seated immediately.

Eat at the counter. The atmosphere isn't as great, but you'll get quick service (and learn the life history of the guy parked on the next stool).

True Story

A Vegas blackjack dealer's cousin came to town. She wanted to see a show, so the dealer gave her a show guide. "Pick the show you want to see," the dealer told her. Her cousin scanned the pages.

Caesars Palace	Johnny Mathis	(Dark Monday)
Bally's	Paul Anka	(Dark Wednesday)
MGM Grand	Wayne Newton	(Dark Tuesday)
Desert Inn	Don Rickles	(Dark Sunday)
Mirage	Siegfried & Roy	(Dark Thursday)

"I wanna see Dark!" the cousin said. "He's playing everywhere!"

How can I avoid long lines elsewhere?

Check into your hotel at mid-morning. (Check-in can take up to an hour on a weekend afternoon.) Mid-morning is also a perfect time to avoid lines at the slot club or gift redemption counter. If you still encounter a line, exclaim loudly, "Hey! I just saw Madonna in the coffee shop!"

A woman tourist asked a casino employee where she could get a cup of coffee. The employee suggested a nearby bar. "Oh, yes," the woman said. "I see the coffee, but I thought that was just for drunks."

What's the secret to getting the best room rates in Las Vegas?

When you call your favorite hotel to make reservations, ask if there are any specials being offered. The hotel's nationwide toll-free number won't volunteer that information. Or let's say you check into your hotel and find that a discounted room rate is being offered that you didn't know about. Just tell the clerk you want your room at the lower price. A hotel vice-president once told me that in such cases, you'll get the same discount.

Millie Ball, travel editor of the *New Orleans Times-Picayune*, likes package deals that include airfare and hotels but don't require much advance notice. "Packages are often cheaper than airfare alone," she writes, so sometimes people buy a package deal just to get a cheaper plane flight and then book a nicer hotel once they get to town. They're still money ahead.

To get the cheapest airfare, book your tickets well in advance. A Southwest Airlines ticket agent told me, "The further away you book, the better fare you get." He said the magic number is 21 days. "If you book 21 days in advance, you'll get the cheapest fare we've got."

Look for fare wars. If one airline is offering cut-rate prices on particular routes, other airlines will usually follow suit.

Make reservations early in the morning. Airlines use this slow period to fill seats that haven't been sold or seats that were booked and never paid for. To get a good seat on an airliner, fly when nobody else wants to, such as early morning or late night.

How do the hotels decide which room I get?

If you ask for a particular room or wing of the hotel, or if you request a non-smoking room, the hotel will do its best to please you. However, most guests don't ask, and so they're assigned to rooms at random. If the hotel isn't sold out, it will usually cluster guests close to each other, and the reason for this is so that housekeepers can clean the rooms more efficiently.

Want a room with a view? Ask for it, but don't make the mistake one first-time tourist did at the Bellagio. She asked the reservation clerk for a room with an ocean view. Las Vegas is in the desert, remember?

When you make reservations, ask for a confirmation number and get the name of the hotel employee to whom you are speaking. Better yet, have the hotel send you your confirmation by letter. That way, you have a written record of your reservation and it will save time when you check in. A friend of mine made a reservation on the Internet, paying $600 up front for his room. When he checked in, the hotel had no record of his room reservation, and charged him another $600. The Internet may be fine for some things, but I wouldn't use it for getting a hotel room. You're better off talking to someone who actually works there.

If your room isn't up to your expectations, call downstairs and complain. Don't wait until you check out. Some hotels will upgrade your room or comp your breakfast simply because you voiced a complaint. If you really want to get another room, flush all your towels down the commode. Just kidding, but one man actually did that on a cruise ship, backing up the sewer line for the whole ship.

How many rooms does a maid clean each day, and how long does it take her to clean each room?

On the average, a maid cleans from 14 to 17 rooms a day, and spends about 20 minutes in each room. Here's the official breakdown:

Five minutes to make the bed, six minutes to clean the bathtub, six minutes to vacuum the carpet, 45 seconds to remove the selector knob on the television set, 15 seconds to set the clock back three hours, one minute to rig the curtains so they won't close all the way, and one minute to turn up the ringer volume on the telephone full blast.

A friend of mine from Minnesota always gives his maid a $20 tip the minute he checks into his room. This guarantees him extra bottles of shampoo and skin cream, the fluffiest towels, and such extras as unopened soft drinks, wine, beer, and fruit drinks that have been left behind by other departing guests. Otherwise, all this stuff is thrown away.

How can I get a room when a hotel says it's sold out?

Try using a travel agent. He has more clout because he does business with the hotel on a regular basis. In other words, he's probably getting a kickback, so make him work for it.

Can I book a room in a Las Vegas hotel if I'm under 21?

No, you have to be 21 years of age, or have an adult with you when you register.

What if I want to stay in my room past check-out time?

Call the front desk and ask for a late check-out. If the hotel is not completely booked for the following night, you can usually keep your room for two or three extra hours at no additional cost.

> **Always get the name of the person who comps you for late check-out or anything else. That way, if you're charged later, you can go right back to the person who comped you.**

What if I have a complaint in the casino?

Nobody knows if you're upset about something unless you tell somebody, and today each casino wants to keep you happy (so they can keep you from going someplace else). If something happens at a table game, complain immediately. The casino is so anxious to keep the game moving that they'll do anything within reason to pacify you.

When you complain, don't lose your temper. Voice your complaint in a friendly manner, and you'll probably get the matter resolved immediately. Holler at the top of your voice, and you're going to make everyone else mad, too.

> *"For the most part, all our floor executives aim to solve problems in a way that will satisfy the customer. For example, we're dealing with people who say that they really didn't want a hit in blackjack, but the dealer gave them one anyway and busted their hand. And we're just as frequently asked to cool off a customer who says the dealer either underpaid his hand, or didn't pay it at all. In nine-tenths of these disputes, and assuming there's no crookedness going on, we solve the matter in the patron's favor."*
>
> Rio Casino Manager

Courtesy is the number one priority in every casino. The way one vice-president explained it to me over cocktails in his palatial mansion (after I finished waxing his Rolls) was, "Put yourself in a customer's shoes. He's spent two hours packing, another hour getting to the airport, five hours flying to Las Vegas, another 45 minutes getting to the hotel in a cab, and 20 minutes checking in. Then he walks into the casino, and a dealer gives him a dirty look because he did something wrong. It ruins the player's entire impression of the casino, and we're lucky if he ever comes back again."

Former Caesars Palace executive Andrea DeWitte shares the following story.

A woman called the hotel recently and asked to speak to Mr. Perkle.

"I'm sorry," Andrea replied. "There's nobody here by that name."

"Well, of course there is," the woman said. "He's your casino manager."

"Are you sure you have the right hotel?"

"This is Caesars Palace, isn't it?"

"Yes, but we don't have a Mr. Perkle working here."

"Well, I've got a letter from him on Caesars Palace stationery."

"And what is the letter in regards to?"

"My husband and I had a bad experience in the showroom. Mr. Perkle wrote me a letter saying to call him the next time I was coming to Las Vegas and he would make it up to us."

"Which show was that?"

"It was the Red Skelton show."

"Red Skelton? When did you see this show?"

"In June. I've got the program right here. June 7th . . . 1982."

In one casino, all the dealers were required to take a mandatory class on customer service. After the class was over, one of the newly-indoctrinated dealers was at his post at the dice table when a woman began to play. "Where are you from?" the dealer asked her politely.

"Tucson," she replied.

He smiled warmly, then asked her, "Did those killer bees get there yet?"

Where can I find some of the best bargains in Las Vegas?

Most casinos have special promotions from time to time that include everything from room rate discounts to two-for-one meals and shows, free coin rolls with buy-ins, and free play coupons. If you're a member of a slot club, news of these specials will be mailed right to your home. To find out about other great bargains around town, I suggest a subscription to *Las Vegas Advisor*. It features a top-ten list, a Pocketbook of Values booklet, and other special discounts for subscribers (1-800-244-2224).

When is the worst time to come to Las Vegas?

On holidays, while a convention is in town, and during big sporting events such as the Super Bowl, the NCAA basketball tournament, or a championship prize fight. Weekdays are always easier to book, and you get your best rates Monday through Thursday.

Best time to come is during the month of June (weddings and graduations keep a lot of people away), the middle of summer, immediately after a holiday, and the two weeks right before Christmas.

Where should I stay?

If you're pinching pennies, get on the telephone and start calling those 800 numbers. Every hotel in Las Vegas has one. Make reservations before you come; 88% of the people do. Ask about specials. Some hotels won't volunteer that information unless you ask. If you really want to do it right, make reservations at one of the following resorts: Caesars Palace ($$$), Treasure Island ($$$), Mirage ($$$), Bally's ($$$), MGM Grand ($$$), New York-New York ($$), Monte Carlo ($$), Imperial Palace ($), Harrah's ($$), Tropicana ($$$), Flamingo Hilton ($$), Barbary Coast ($), Aladdin ($$), Excalibur ($$), Luxor ($$), Paris-Las Vegas ($$), Venetian ($$$), or Bellagio ($$$$). They're all within a mile of each other, and you won't spend all your time in traffic.

Incidentally, *Las Vegas Advisor* took a survey on which hotels its readers liked the best. The top ten, in order, were Mirage, Horseshoe, Flamingo Hilton, Golden Nugget, Four Queens, Rio, Caesars Palace, Stardust, Bally's, and Harrah's.

My Uncle Frank submitted his own top ten list: Dunes, Landmark, Sands, Silver Slipper, Castaways, Mint, El Rancho, Thunderbird, Hacienda, and Marina. As you can see, Uncle Frank hasn't been to Las Vegas in quite a while.

What about RV parks?

There are plenty of good RV parks around Las Vegas. The best are at Sam's Town, Circus Circus, and the Primm Valley Resort RV Village in Primm, Nevada. Make reservations before you come, and that way you won't be cruising all over town in a 35-foot rig looking for a place to camp.

As a former RV owner, here are some other tips I've learned from past experiences:

- Make sure your TV antenna is lowered before leaving your RV site. (My cost for a new antenna was $36.51.)
- Make sure your awning has been retracted before leaving your RV site. (My cost for a new awning was $714.92.)
- Make sure your propane tank has been shut off be fore lighting your pipe. (My cost for a new motor home was $19,371.14.)

I can never find a water fountain in the casino. How do I get a glass of water?

Water? You've flown 1,800 miles to get to Las Vegas and now you want a glass of water? Well . . . just go to a bar and ask for it. There's no charge.

How do I get a cocktail while I'm playing?

Tell the dealer or change attendant that you want a drink. She'll tell her supervisor, and he'll call a cocktail waitress. Drinks are complimentary while you're playing, but if you want to see the waitress again it's a good idea to give her a tip. Other suggestions:

Ask for liquor by brand names. Otherwise, you'll usually get the cheapest hooch in the joint. This doesn't always work, however. A bartender in one casino said if somebody orders Crown Royal and Coke, they'll get Canadian Club and Coke. Canadian Club is cheaper, and nobody drinking this concoction can tell the difference anyway.

If you're drinking at a casino bar, ask for a roll of quarters. Most bartenders will comp you to at least one free drink if they think you're going to play the slots while you're drinking.

A well-heeled gambler, with a credit line of $125,000, took a $10,000 marker in a plush Vegas casino. He immediately ordered two shots of Louis XIII, a French cognac that goes for $1,500 a bottle. This stuff would cost you and me $125 a glass, but he just signed the tab to his room, where anything he ordered was free. Later the man ordered two more shots, and then two more! At $125 a glass, this came to $750, plus a $25 tip for the cocktail waitress each time she brought him a round. The man wound up losing $30,000—so that cognac wound up costing him $5,000 a glass!

Can you tip the cocktail waitress with casino chips, or must you tip with cash?

They'll take anything: chips, cash, stocks, bonds. The only time a cocktail waitress will trade a chip for cash is at roulette, since there is no dollar value on roulette chips.

What is the most popular alcoholic beverage ordered by customers?

I'll give you a quiz, and let's see if you come up with the right answer:

> Beer
> Bourbon and water
> Screwdriver
> Gin and tonic
> Wine

If you said screwdriver, you're right. According to bartenders and cocktail waitresses, more people order a screwdriver than any other drink, with Bloody Mary a distant second. Why? "It's because people don't like to mix their liquors," a waitress said. "If they start with vodka, they'll stick with vodka all day."

What is a "floater"?

A "floater" is a cocktail made of mix, with only a thin layer of booze floating on top. It's for tipsy gamblers who insist on more drinks. This way, their first taste is of alcohol, and after that they don't know the difference anyway.

What are the liquor laws in Las Vegas?

Unlike other states with their "last call for alcohol," there are no closing hours in Vegas. Although drinking laws in Nevada are liberal, penalties for inebriated drivers are not. So if you're drinking, hand your car keys to somebody else—preferably somebody you know.

As a casino employee, what is your pet peeve?

People who point. I've been jabbed in the ear, the nose, the mouth, and all points south by people pointing their fingers when someone else asks for directions. Those aren't glasses I'm wearing; they're protective goggles!

How do I make reservations to see a show?

If you're a high roller, simply tell V.I.P. Services what show you want to see. For the 99.08% of us who are not high rollers, see the concierge or go to the hotel's ticket booth. Many of these booths have tickets for virtually every show in town, so you can usually get reservations without even leaving your hotel. On the night of the show, plan to get there about 45 minutes before showtime.

Should I go to the "Invited Guest Line" or the "Seating Line" at the showroom?

Go to the "Seating Line" with all the other huddled masses. The "Invited Guest Line"—or "V.I.P. Line" as it is sometimes called—is only for high rollers and others with complimentary tickets.

What's the secret of getting a good seat or a booth at a Las Vegas show?

Most shows are booked through professional ticket agencies like Ticketron, so tipping the showroom captain will only get you a better seat right before the show starts and only if better seating is still available. Here's a safer (and more inexpensive) way of getting a better seat or a booth, as shared by my good friend Bob Olsen of Boston. Go to the hotel where the show you want to see is playing. Ask to see a diagram of the seating, and have the ticket seller show you on the diagram where your seat is. If you don't like the location, ask him for a better seat or a booth. If nothing is available for that night, then ask him for a booth the following night, or the night after. Bob says it's worked for him every time.

I can never find a restroom or a telephone in the casino. Why don't the casinos put up signs to show where everything is?

There are usually signs in the casino, but they're hard to find, too. Your best bet is to ask an employee. If they can't tell you, nobody can.

Of course, that won't always work. Take the lady who walked up to an elderly dealer in the casino.

"How do you get out of here?" she asked him.

The dealer scratched his head ruefully. "Lady, I've been trying to figure that out for the last 15 years!"

Besides casinos, what are the most popular tourist destinations in and near Las Vegas?

In Las Vegas, the top attractions (in no particular order) are Adventuredome at Circus Circus, circus acts at Circus Circus, King Tut's tomb and museum at Luxor, the Bellagio Gallery of Fine Art, the Liberace Museum on East Tropicana, Grand Canal gondola rides at Venetian, Wet 'n' Wild on the north end of the Strip, "Star Trek: The Experience" at Las Vegas Hilton, "Race for Atlantis" inside the Forum Shops at Caesars Palace, roller coasters at New York-New York and Sahara, and the scariest ride in town: the Big Shot at Strastosphere. Remember this, though. The odds of dying on a thrill ride are only 1 in 200 million. How many people have ridden the Big Shot? Exactly 199,999,999 people. (So maybe you better wait a week.)

The best of the theme restaurants is Planet Hollywood (inside the Forum Shops at Caesars). Owners include Bruce Willis, Demi Moore, Sylvester Stallone, and Arnold Schwarzeneggergrooberloober. You're bound to see a costume or prop from one of your favorite movies, and

afterwards you can buy a jacket, T-shirt, or Rolaids com-
memorating your visit.

Among tourists who visit nearby areas, 67% were
most likely to visit Hoover Dam, followed by the Grand
Canyon, Lake Mead, Laughlin, and Death Valley.

Is there a neon sign graveyard in Las Vegas?

Yes there is, but the original graveyard is not open to
the public. However, half a dozen of those famous old
signs are in an open-air museum as part of the Fremont
Street Experience. These galleries, as they are called, are
free to view, 24 hours a day, and best seen at night when
they're lit up. You might see the Hacienda Hotel horse and
rider (five stories tall) or the original Aladdin's Lamp from
1966, as the signs are changed periodically. Incidentally,
construction is underway for an outdoor Neon Museum
near Cashman Center that will feature a more extensive
sign boneyard and cultural center.

How do I get coupons for free merchandise in Las Vegas?

Funbooks and coupons are usually available at hotel
welcome centers and inside non-casino motels around
town. Or check inside one of those freebie magazines you
can find in any hotel lobby. In one recent issue of
Tourguide, I found the following: Free deck of cards at
Slots-A-Fun, free slot pull at the Riviera, free hat at
Fitzgeralds, free sun visor at Imperial Palace, $16 in buffet
discounts at the Stardust, two-for-one ticket at the 3-D
cinema ride at Caesars Forum Shops, free deck of cards at
the Stardust, and free souvenirs at Silver City and San
Remo.

Some travel agents also distribute coupons and funbooks for Vegas casinos, so ask for them if you book your
trip through either a travel agent or package tour agent.
One of the best all-time Vegas freebies was a porcelain

coffee mug with the Sands logo on it. It retailed for $7, and the Sands gave away 5 million of them. Let's see, 5 million X $7 = $35,000,000. Don't bother going to the Sands for yours. The Sands went belly-up shortly after this promotion began.

What are other ways I can economize while I'm in Las Vegas?

- Ask the hotel for a refrigerator. There's usually no charge for this service, and now you can keep drinks, fruit, sandwich meats, and leftovers in your room.

- Bring a small coffee maker with you, and save more money by not using room service every morning.

- Take in a lounge show instead of a big showroom extravaganza. There's a lot of great talent in Vegas lounges, and most have no cover charge or drink minimum. Just look at some of those who got their start in Las Vegas lounge shows: Kenny Rogers, Don Rickles, Shecky Greene, the Mary Kaye Trio, Louis Prima, and Keely Smith. And the stars of tomorrow are in those lounges right now!

- Catch your favorite sporting event in a casino sports book. The chairs are comfortable, the drinks are free (sometimes they even have free eats), and you don't have to make a bet unless you want to.

- Use the CAT (Citizens Area Transit) bus system or trolleys to get around town. The trolleys look like old San Francisco cable cars, and stop right at the entrances to all casinos on the Strip.

How can I *really* economize on my trip?

Here are some suggestions from my Uncle Frank. Hitchhike everywhere you go. Don't tip anybody. Bring a metal detector with you. (Uncle Frank claims he found a cup of nickels, a camera, two brass buttons, a cigarette lighter, and a paper clip.) When you eat in a casino buffet, wear a large overcoat with plenty of inside pockets. And never check out of your hotel room empty-handed.

What can I take from my hotel room?

Each year the average Vegas resort spends around $35,000 on facial soap, a like amount on bath soap, $90,0000 on shampoo and conditioner, $30,000 on bath gel, and $45,000 on vanity packs—and it's yours for the taking. A hotel general manager put it this way. "You can take anything that starts with an S, except sheets." So that includes soap, shower caps, shoeshine cloths, shampoo, stationery, and sewing kits. Leave everything else, or you might find it charged to your credit card.

Everything seems more expensive in Las Vegas nowadays. What happened to all the cheap rooms and cheap meals?

Give me a minute while I climb on top of my soapbox. Now give me another minute to catch my breath. Okay, here's the situation. Visitor surveys show that the rate of hard-core gamblers (those who visit Vegas six or more times a year) is declining at a rate of 30% a year. That's because there are more casino options closer to home. On the other hand, first-time visitors and families are increasing at about the same rate of 30%. Since these people don't gamble as much, the casino jacks up its room rates to maintain the same margin of profit.

As far as meals go, Las Vegas is still famous for its cheap buffets. Many of the other casino restaurants are leased operations that don't participate in casino revenues. Therefore, their pricing reflects the true cost of operations like it does everywhere else in the country.

My advice to you is to stay in a motel close to the

Strip, or at a downtown hotel where room rates are within reason. Skip the fancy restaurants, and eat where the locals do. If you're not sure where to go or what to see, ask somebody who works in a casino. Most casino employees would be flattered if you asked their opinion.

My advice to the casinos is to get back to the basics that made Las Vegas the world's most famous value-oriented destination. Bring back the lounge shows. Lower the room rates. Cut the price of showroom tickets. Comp anybody who gambles to the buffet. (After all, when you eat in a buffet, you're *still* gambling.) Treat your employees and customers like human beings instead of statistics. I guarantee you'll be the most successful casino operation in the world.

Would somebody help me down off my soapbox now? I'm getting a nose bleed.

I remember seeing Bonnie and Clyde's death car on a trip to the Las Vegas area a few years ago. Is it still around?

Unfortunately, yes. The car in which outlaws Bonnie and Clyde were executed Louisiana-style in 1934 is on display at the Primm Valley Resort at the California-Nevada state line. You can also see Clyde Barrow's "death shirt," which former casino owner Gary Primm bought at a recent auction for $75,000. No word yet on where you can see Clyde's death socks and underwear.

Do they still have bingo in Las Vegas?

As this goes to print, bingo is played at almost two dozen Vegas casinos. Unfortunately, they change from day to day. Your best bet is to pick up a complimentary copy of *What's On* magazine at your hotel, and check to see who's got bingo this week. Also listed are times and prizes. Advantage to playing bingo: The casino rarely makes a profit on the games. Disadvantage: Long waits between sessions.

Where can I go horseback riding?

In Wyoming! But if you're already in Las Vegas, head on up to Mountain T Ranch (55 miles north of town on Kyle Canyon Road). Trail rides last from 1 to 6 hours, and will run you anywhere from $20 to $100. Closer in is Cowboy Trail Rides, with horseback rides at Red Rock Canyon and other scenic spots. The most popular of these rides takes place at sunset. Afterwards, you're treated to a tasty barbecue around a campfire. For more information, call 1-800-MY BUTT HURTS.

Where can I go ice skating?

The Santa Fe Casino, in northwest Las Vegas, has a professional ice skating arena (200 by 85 feet). It's available for open skating, private and group lessons, and amateur and semi-professional hockey.

How about spas and workout facilities?

There are complete spas and workout facilities at Bally's, Caesars Palace, Harrah's, Imperial Palace, Luxor, MGM Grand, Mandalay Bay, Monte Carlo, Riviera, and Tropicana. The daily fee averages about $20.

Where can I find a good arcade for the kids?

Most major casinos have arcades, but some are better than others. The most popular ones, according to Anthony Curtis in Bargain City, are at Circus Circus, Excalibur, and Luxor.

The only problem is that they let kids in them.

What should I do if my car breaks down in the desert?

If you decide to explore the desert, let a friend know where you're going and when you plan to return. If your car breaks down, stay near it and wait for help. If you must leave your car, here are some suggestions from the Boulder Outdoor Survival School, and some of my own.

Boulder Survival School	Me
Zigzagging across a steep hill conserves more energy than climbing straight up.	Go around it.
If you can't spot any insects or other life in a water source, steer clear. It could be poisonous.	*If you spot insects or other life in a water source, steer clear. It could be dangerous.*
To determine how much daylight is left, hold a fist up to the western horizon and stack fists on top of one another up to the sun's level in the sky. Each fist represents about one hour of sunlight.	Look at your wristwatch.
Game animals know best. Their trails form the easiest, most direct route to safety.	*Call for help on your cellular phone*

What is the average salary of casino employees?

The president of a resort on the Las Vegas Strip makes a minimum of $300,000 a year, with amenities that might include a home, limousine, stock options, and club memberships. Casino managers earn in the neighborhood of $125,000. Casino hosts average $100,000. Shift managers make about $80,000. Floor supervisors earn a little over half that. Union workers make scale plus tips. Non-union workers usually make minimum wage plus tips.

How does this compare with jobs outside the casino industry? Doctors make about $4 million a year, dentists $3 million, lawyers $2 million, and plumbers $1 million.

How much should I tip when I'm in a casino?

That's a matter of personal choice, and there are no hard-set rules. If a dealer has been helpful and friendly, give him a $1 or $5 chip occasionally, or make a bet for the dealer alongside your bet. You'll have a friend for life, and he may even follow you home. The rule of thumb for other casino personnel:

- **Cocktail waitresses or bartenders**—$1 a round for two people.
- **Valet attendants**—$1 to $2.
- **Doormen**—$1 to $2, and another buck a bag if he unloads your car.
- **Cab drivers**—Fifteen percent of the total fare, never less than $1.
- **Maids**—$2 to $3 a night, left daily so the person cleaning your room is the one who gets it.
- **Bellhops**—$1 a bag.
- **Keno runners**—$1 occasionally, more if you accidentally win something.
- **Slot attendants**—Two to five percent of jackpot winnings.
- **Buffet**—$1 for each person.
- **Showroom servers**—$5 to $10 for a drinks-only show, $10 to $20 for a dinner show.

- **Restaurant waiter**—Ten to 20 percent of the total bill.
- **Maître d'**— $10 to $20.
- **Mayor of Las Vegas**—$50.
- **Governor of Nevada**—$100.

12
Trivia

Why aren't there any clocks in the casinos?

There are clocks in the casinos; you just have to know where to look. In most casinos, you simply enter the coffee shop, exit through the kitchen door, then walk down a dimly-lit stairway to the basement. Now go past the wardrobe department, the purchasing office, and the first aid room. Off to the right you'll see the time office. Inside is a time clock where the employees punch in and out. It'll give you the correct time.

How do I get a job in Las Vegas?

It's not as hard as you might think. At last report, there were over a million residents in Las Vegas, and consequently the city is experiencing the growing pains of any other metropolitan area. Therefore, there's a big demand for drug counselors, policemen, prison guards, probation officers, judges, pawn shop attendants, flop house night clerks, compulsive gambling counselors, and Alcoholics Anonymous volunteers.

But seriously, if you're entertaining the idea of moving to Las Vegas, there are scores of employment opportunities—and most of these jobs come with benefit packages including medical, dental, vision, and life insurance. In addition, many casinos offer educational assistance, so you can get an even better job!

I called the Caesars Palace Job Hotline one afternoon and found job openings for the following positions: security dispatcher, assistant beverage manager, casino account representative, casino collection clerk, computer operator, direct marketing clerk, administrative entertainment assistant, clerk-typist, executive pastry chef, housekeeping night shift supervisor, inventory control supervisor, office manager for convention sales, PBX operator, mailroom runner, catering sales manager, merchandising sales associate, sales reservation agent, casino development secretary, salon receptionist, catering secretary, security officer (full time and part time), and international marketing representative for the Middle East. That was just at Caesars Palace!

PART OF THE JOB DESCRIPTION FOR DICE PIT MANAGER AT ONE LAS VEGAS CASINO:
"Must be able to move through the pit and stand for long periods of time. Must be able to see to do paperwork and to provide supervisory observations."

(They could have added: "Must be under 100 years of age.")

Hotels are constantly in search of housekeeping personnel. Maids make around $10 an hour, plus union benefits.

Casinos can't find enough change people to man the slot machines, and with tips the job averages out to about $75 a day.

Are you a retired cop or ex-serviceman? You might consider becoming a casino security guard. You get to carry a flashlight, nightstick, handcuffs, two-way radio, and all kinds of other neat stuff. You'll do a lot of walking (about 6 miles a day) and you'll probably start out at around $8 an hour. After a couple of years, though, your pay can climb to as high as $110 a day.

Here's a real sleeper that few people know about. Massage therapy! Many casinos now offer this service, and therapists can make anywhere from $20 to $50 an hour. You'll have to take an eight-month course at a cost of around $6,000, but you're in big demand once you get your license.

Cocktail waitresses make about $7 an hour now, but their whole paycheck usually goes to the I.R.S. because of taxes they pay on each drink served. Still, this is one of the best tip jobs in Vegas—which makes it hard to get your shapely foot in the door. Other drawbacks: scanty outfits, the probability you'll be working in slots or keno until you establish seniority, and your first name has to end in an "*i.*"

Most Vegas newcomers want to be casino dealers, because that's where the big money is. A dealer in a top casino (Caesars Palace, MGM Grand, Tropicana, Hilton properties, MGM resorts) can make upwards of $60,000 a year in tips alone.

You'll have to go to a dealers school first and learn the proper way to deal. There's always a big demand for crap dealers since this is the hardest game to learn.   Better yet, learn two games, or even three. That makes you even more valuable.

As a dealer, you should also know how to "cut" chips. You'll be handling chips constantly: paying bets, taking bets, making change. There's an art to cutting chips into stacks, and then "sizing" into them with other chips. Buy a stack of poker chips and practice, practice, practice. If you plan to become a dealer, this will be time well spent. You'll also have to get a sheriff's card, which must be carried on your person while working. No ex-felon can get one. (Sorry, Uncle Frank.)

Drawbacks: Standing on your feet for eight hours a

day, having smoke blown in your face, getting splashed by overturned drinks, being subjected to verbal abuse by sore losers and intoxicated gamblers, being propositioned, working every holiday and weekend for the rest of your life, then having someone walk up to your table and say, "How come you people never smile?"

> **To find out what job openings are available, call the casino's "Job Hotline."**
>
> **If a particular job interests you, go to the casino personnel office (or Human Resources) and fill out an application. Qualifications are usually listed on the personnel office bulletin board. Take a professional résumé if you have one. This will set your application apart from the scores of others.**

What's the difference between praying in a church and praying in a casino?

When you pray in a casino, you really mean it.

Has gambling ever been halted in a Las Vegas casino?

On Monday, November 25, 1963, gambling came to a stop for three hours in memory of President John Kennedy. That same day there was no entertainment on the Strip from 7 a.m. until midnight, the longest talent blackout in the history of Las Vegas. There was also a minute of silence when Martin Luther King was assassinated, and a minute of silence in all Howard Hughes resorts when the billionaire recluse died.

Marquee lights were dimmed for a minute at the passing of Frank Sinatra (1998), Dean Martin (1995), and Sammy Davis Jr. (1990).

I hear a lot of slang expressions when I'm in Las Vegas. Please explain.

For some strange reason, there are a lot of slang words used in casinos. Maybe it all goes back to when gambling was illegal, and patrons of such dens of iniquity used code words to keep more righteous citizens from knowing what the heck they were talking about.

Another reason is that casino workers like to shorten the names of everything whenever possible. This is because most dealers only talk to one another while they're working, which is known as "crossfiring," and that's one of the pit boss's biggest peeves. By using short words in place of long words, a dealer can crossfire for quite a while before the pit boss catches him and has him executed.

Here's a glossary of other popular casino terms:

Agent—A cheater's outside confederate. Also the sly and cunning individual who rakes 15% right off the top of any writer's meager profits.

Apron—Garment worn around the dealer's waist, usually imprinted with the casino logo.

Audition—Dealing in front of a supervisor for a possible job opening.

BJ—Abbreviated term for "blackjack."

Barber pole—A stack of chips with various denominations all mixed together.

Basket—A three-number roulette bet on any of these: 0, 00, 1, 2, or 3.

Beef—Argument or dispute in the casino.

Blacks—$100 chips.

Greens—$25 dollar chips.

Reds—$5 chips. Also known as "nickels."

Silver—Dollar tokens. Also known as "iron."

Bird Game—Twenty-five cent table. (In other words, this game is for the birds.)

Bones—Dice.

Book—Race or sports book.

Bowl—Dice container.

Boxcars—A twelve at the dice table.

Boxman—The casino supervisor who monitors the dice game. He also puts all the money in the casino drop box, hence the title "boxman."

Break—The employee's coveted rest period.

Break In—A novice dealer.

Bust—A showgirl's greatest attribute, or when you or the blackjack dealer goes over 21.

Buy In—The amount of paper money with which a player enters a game.

Cage—Casino cashier's area.

Cecil—A $100 bill.

Checks—Casino chips.

Chung—Marker signifying "banker" at pai gow.

Clerk—A good dealer, as opposed to:

Lumpy—A bad dealer.

Clipper—A cash forger who pastes or "clips" the corners of $20 bills onto $1 bills, and then tries to pass them off.

Comp—Anything you get for free in the casino.

Cooler—A pre-arranged deck of cards substituted for another deck by crooked players.

Counter—A blackjack player who keeps track of the cards, makes his bets accordingly, then gets hustled out the door by two big security guards.

Crew—The dealers on a dice or baccarat game.

Crossroader—Former cheater turned respectable, or vice versa.

Croupier—Fancy word for a dealer. Use this word in Las Vegas and you'll be laughed out of town.

Cut Card—The plastic card used by a blackjack player to cut the cards after the shuffle.

Dead Game—A table game with no players, as opposed to:

Full Game—A casino game with all seats occupied.

Dive Bomber—Also known as a "stooper," this deadbeat prowls race and sports books looking for winning tickets that have accidentally been thrown away.

Double Deck—A blackjack game using two decks of cards.

Double Down—To double your original bet at a blackjack game, taking one additional card.

Drop—The bills that the dealer drops in a gaming table's money slot (or drop box). Drop is also the hold percentage on each casino game.

Duke—A big hand at the dice table.

Early Out—The lucky employee who gets the last break before quittin' time.

Exacta—A bet at the race track requiring the player to pick the winner and place horse in the exact order of finish. Another popular bet is the "trifecta," where the player picks the winner, place horse, and show horse in the same order. This is followed by the "bankrupta," which is when the player tears up all his losing exacta and trifecta tickets.

Extra Board—List of part-time dealers who are available when needed. It's probably the worst job in the casino.

Eye in the Sky—Overhead casino surveillance.

Fill—The replenishment of the dealer's rack (or chip tray).

Flat Bed Store—A crooked casino.

Floater—Relief dealer assigned to give extra breaks.

Flush—Five cards of the same suit in a poker hand.

George—A player who bets for the dealers, as opposed to:

Stiff—A player who doesn't give anybody anything anytime anywhere anyhow. A stiff is also a bad hand at any card game.

Goose—The device that spits out the balls in a keno game.

Hand In—A tip from a player.

Handle—The amount of money wagered by players in any casino game.

Hard Count—The casino's count of coins taken from slot machines, as opposed to:

Soft Count—The casino's count of paper money.

Hardways—Any double (except aces or twelve) at the dice table. Caution: As Confucius once said, "He who bets hardways will soon fall on hard times."

Heat—Close scrutiny or constant criticism by a pit boss.

High Roller—A well-heeled gambler. Also known as a "whale."

High Low—A bet on aces and twelve at the dice table.

Hole Card—The card dealt face down to the blackjack dealer.

Host—Casino liaison between the player and the hotel.

Hopper—The coin bank inside a slot machine.

Hot Seat—The person sitting to the dealer's right at a blackjack table. Also called "third base."

House—The casino.

Hustling—The act of openly soliciting tips from a player.

Insurance—The opportunity to insure your bet at a blackjack game when the dealer turns over an ace by placing up to half your original bet on the table's Insurance line. If the dealer has a blackjack, you're paid 2 to 1 for your insurance bet, thereby "insuring" your original wager. If the dealer doesn't have a blackjack, you lose your insurance bet. (Not recommended.)

Juice—The art of getting a job in the casino with a friend's help. It's a lot harder to do than it used to be, since prospective employees now have to be cleared by the Personnel Office, Corporate Security, the Gaming Control Board, the FBI, the Church of Latter Day Saints, and your former high school principal.

Ladder Man—Used in early casinos, this was the casino observer who watched the action on the floor from a nice big chair atop a ladder. The practice of using ladder men was discontinued, however, because most of them fell asleep in those nice big chairs.

Lammer—A button used to signify certain bets on the dice table.

Layout—The felt covering the gaming table.

Line Bet—A bet on the pass line at craps.

Mechanic—A card or dice cheat.

Miss Out—End of a hand at the dice table.

Mucker—Dealer who sorts chips at roulette game. Also called an "apron."

Paddle—A plastic device with a rubber tip used by casino personnel to push money into the drop box.

Paint—A face card.

Parlay—To bet back all your winnings at a table game. Also a multi-game bet on a sports ticket.

Pit—Any area in the casino where gaming tables are located.

Press—Doubling your original bet.

Puck—The round disc marking the point on a dice table.

Push—A tie between the dealer and the player, in which no money changes hands.

Rack—The rectangular metal tray on the gaming table where casino chips are kept, or the apparatus on which your body will be stretched if you're caught cheating.

Rake—The amount the casino takes from each pot in a poker game. This can be as high as 10%, but usually there's a limit of $3 per pot.

Score—For a player, it means hitting it big at the tables. For a dealer, it means getting a lot of tips, as opposed to:

Blank—Not making any tips.

Shill—A person who pretends to be gambling so that other people will gamble.

Shoe—The plastic box containing anywhere from 4 to 8 decks of cards. In Texas casinos, this is called a boot. (Ouch.)

Sleeper—Money inadvertently left behind at a casino game by a player.

Snake Eyes—Two aces at the dice table.

Snapper—A blackjack.

Soft Hand—Any hand in blackjack with an ace as one of the cards.

Split—To make two hands out of one hand in blackjack by splitting any pair. Remember, though, you have to match your original bet on each hand.

Stickman—The dealer who calls the dice rolls at a crap table.

Store—A nice casino, as compared to:

Toilet—A bad casino.

Straight—Five cards in order at poker (5-6-7-8-9).

Sub—Device used by a crooked dealer to steal money.

Toke—A tip for any casino employee.

Toke Box—The box where the dealers keep their tips.

Two Way Bet—A bet for you and the dealer.

Vigorish—Commission paid on winning bets.

Wheel—A roulette wheel.

Okay, here's your test. Translate the following sentence:

"I was playing BJ in this toilet when the stiff in the hot seat split paints on a full game and got two snappers."

Congratulations. Now you know as much as a pit boss.

The other day I lost $500 at the blackjack table, and I got so angry I hit the dealer over the head with a 9 iron. Should I apologize?

Of course. The shot called for a sand wedge.

Why is there a yellow line on the floor in the casino executive offices?

It's so the people coming to work late don't bump into the people going home early.

Is there a state lottery in Nevada?

No. The 35th session of the Nevada Legislature, which approved legalized gambling and quickie divorces, worded the law so that a state lottery would be illegal. The reasoning was that a lottery would compete with casino gambling, and the law was never changed.

Of course, that doesn't mean that people in Nevada don't play the lottery. They do, only they drive 35 miles to the state line and play the California lottery.

Who were the original members of the Rat Pack?

Mighty Mouse (Frank Sinatra), Mickey Mouse (Dean Martin), Minnie Mouse (Peter Lawford), Jerry Mouse (Joey Bishop), Topo Gigio (Sammy Davis Jr.), and the Mouseketeers (Copa Girls).

What is the Nevada Test Site?

The Nevada Test Site, located 65 miles northwest of Las Vegas, is a mammoth testing ground for underground nuclear explosions. The site covers 1,300 square miles, employs 11,000 people, and has an annual budget of $1 billion. The first nuclear test at the Nevada Test Site took place in December of 1950. In those days, no one knew the dangers of radioactivity, and the first series of nuclear tests were aboveground.

According to the Nevada Test Site, there are four reasons for continued nuclear testing: development of new weapons systems, proof testing of stockpiled weapons to assure reliability, development of new safeguards to prevent accidental detonations or unauthorized use of nuclear weapons, and research on the effects of radiation on military hardware. Frankly, though, I think we can put that $1 billion to better use on other things, like inventing a safe cigarette.

What can you tell me about Nellis Air Force Base?

Nellis Air Force Base is located on 11,000 acres north

of the city. Named for Robert Nellis, a Las Vegas fighter pilot who died over Germany during a World War II bombing raid, the air base was shared by the air force and commercial aircraft until 1945. That's when the city bought Crockett's Alamo Airport, which eventually became McCarran International Airport.

Meanwhile, Nellis became the home of the country's largest tactical Air Force Command with over 15,000 military and civilian employees. The most famous group of flyers assigned to Nellis Air Force Base are the Thunderbirds, a precision flying team that puts on about 75 air shows a year and attracts crowds of up to 300,000.

Which celebrities are popular with dealers, and which ones aren't?

According to those who have dealt to celebrities, these were the dealers' favorites: Elvis Presley, Tony Curtis, James Woods, Vanna White, Dean Martin, Sammy Davis Jr., Richard Pryor, John Wayne, Joey Bishop, James Brown, Andrew Dice Clay, Annette Funicello, Clint Eastwood, Drew Carey, Vic Tayback, Jack Klugman, George Peppard, Don Rickles, Magic Johnson, Tommy Hearns, Tim Conway, Dennis Miller, Dustin Hoffman, Tom Cruise, Don Johnson, Joe Pesci, Jerry Van Dyke, Charles Barkley, Ben Affleck, Sugar Ray Leonard, Julia Roberts, and Julio Iglesias. "Julio kissed my hand when he left the table," one blackjack dealer remembered warmly. (She was a female dealer, by the way.)

The worst? Jerry Lewis, Frank Sinatra, Redd Foxx, Robert De Niro, Kenny Rogers, Jimmy Connors, Don Adams, O. J. Simpson, Rodney Dangerfield, Pete Rose, Larry Flynt, Joe Theisman, Dennis Rodman, Tiger Woods, Joe Frazier, Luke Perry, Brett Butler, Bill Cosby, Milton Berle, Bruce Willis, Paul Anka, former Louisiana Governor Edwin Edwards, Scotty Pippin (whose nickname in casinos is "No tippin' Pippin"), and every dealer's top choice as worst celebrity—Diana Ross! "Not only does she never tip," one dealer lamented, "but she also tells the other players not to tip." Another dealer said, "I love the lady's music, especially when she sang with the Supremes, but once she beat me out of $40,000 and never toked me a nickel. Whenever one of her songs come on the radio, I switch immediately to another station."

Speaking of celebrities, I was working at Caesars Palace one day when a familiar-looking man sat down at a Pai Gow poker table. He had jet-black hair and so many face-lifts that every time he blinked his kneecaps went up and down. I walked over to him and said, "Excuse me, but aren't you Eddie Fisher?"

He smiled forlornly and said, "I used to be."

Are there any maps of stars' homes in Las Vegas?

I don't know of any, but quite a few celebrities call Vegas home, including Andre Agassi, Louie Anderson, Paul Anka, Lance Burton, David Cassidy, Geniffer Flowers, Danny Gans, Robert Goulet, B. B. King, Gladys Knight, Jerry Lewis, Rich Little, Greg Maddux, Debbie Reynolds, Kenny Rogers, Siegmund & Freud—er, Siegfried & Roy, Keely Smith, Dick Smothers, Mike Tyson, and yours truly—who lives in a motor home in a gravel pit just off the freeway. The easiest to find are Phyllis McGuire's big place at Alta and Rancho Drives inside the Rancho Circle complex (you can see the tennis courts over the fence), and Wayne Newton's Casa de Shenandoah at the corner of Sunset and Pecos.

What is Nevada's official motto?

"In Odds We Trust."

How many schools are there in Las Vegas?

There are around 185 primary and secondary schools, attended by more than 170,000 students. There's also UNLV (University of Nevada, Las Vegas), which is the largest university in the state, and Community College of Southern Nevada.

How many hospitals are there in Las Vegas?

There are eight acute care hospitals, four hospices, more than 2,000 hospital beds, several licensed nursing homes, and a couple of private psychiatric clinics. The psychiatric clinic where I stayed for eight months was really nice, and I made many lifelong friends—including my agent, editor, publisher, and many of my readers.

How many churches are there in Las Vegas?

Believe it or not, Las Vegas has more churches per capita than any other city in America, with over 500 churches and synagogues for more than 40 faiths.

What is the oldest casino site in Las Vegas?

The Las Vegas Club in downtown Las Vegas sits on the site of the Overland Park Hotel, which opened in 1905. The oldest continually-running casino, however, is the Golden Gate, which opened in 1906.

What was the first casino in Las Vegas?

The Northern Club received the city's first gaming license on March 20, 1931. Today the property, at 15 East Fremont, is known as the Coin Castle.

What was the first casino on the Las Vegas Strip?

It was the Western-themed El Rancho Vegas (now a vacant lot across from the Sahara), which opened in April of 1941 with 63 hotel rooms, a casino, and a 250-seat showroom. The hotel fell on hard times in 1960 and iron-ically burned to the ground that same year. One insider said the fire was choreographed by the same people who produced *Oklahoma*, *Hello Dolly*, and the two Cassius Clay–Sonny Liston fights.

Why is Las Vegas Boulevard called the Strip?

The term was coined by former California cop Guy McAfee, who opened the 91 Club in 1938. People were always asking him where his club was, and he would say, "It's out on the Strip," meaning the road to Los Angeles. This was a carryover from his years in Hollywood, where the original Sunset Strip was located. It's been called the Strip ever since.

Who discovered Las Vegas?

Some say it was Howard Hughes, but let's look in the old history book. The area was long the home of the Anasazi Indians, but the first non-Indian on the scene was a young Mexican scout by the name of Rafael Rivera. He was looking for water off the Old Spanish Trail, and found it in the Las Vegas Valley somewhere between 1830 and 1848. Of course, it wasn't called the Las Vegas Valley then. In fact, it didn't even have a name, but the area resembled a giant meadow. Hence the name Las Vegas, which means "the meadows." Rivera immediately applied for a gaming license, liquor license, cabaret license, hotel license, zone variance, land easement, and commercial building permit—and opened the Riviera Hotel somewhere between 1848 and 1954.

Who was Clark County named for?

It was named for Montana Senator William Andrew Clark (1839–1925). Clark bought the water rights to three artesian springs in the Vegas Valley in 1902, along with 1,800 acres of land. He laid out the townsite of Las Vegas, naming the streets after famous explorers of the West: Fremont, Ogden, Lewis, Clark, and pioneer settler Octavius Gass. Clark paid $55,000 for the land, cut it into lots, and sold each lot at auction for $300—winding up with a quarter of a million dollars and his name on everything in sight.

How many people work in a casino?

It varies, according to the size of the casino. Binion's Horseshoe employs 2,600; Caesars Palace 4,000; and the MGM Grand has a work force of 7,000 people! Twenty-seven percent of Las Vegas' 570,000 employed people work in casinos, and I think the other 73% work for the government.

You have to remember that each Las Vegas resort is like a small city, and every department is an integral part of the overall operation.

Accounting Department—The pulse of the hotel, where all financial transactions are made. Under this department comes General Ledger, where income and expenses are entered; Accounts Payable, where bills are paid; Accounts Receivable, where credit card purchases and personal checks are cleared; and General Auditing, where profit and loss statements for each department are verified.

Casino Cage—The center of all casino transactions, with three sub-departments: Credit Department, where credit is established and markers are recorded; Cashier's Cage, where casino customers are serviced and fills for the table games are made; and the Casino Collections Department, which is made up of three big guys named Rocky, Knuckles, and Lefty.

Purchasing Department—A bookkeeper's nightmare, where all purchases are made. If you want to sell anything to the hotel, from roulette wheels to computers, this is where you go.

Maintenance Department—This is the department that fixes all the roulette wheels and computers that the Purchasing Department bought. Under this department come the army of workers that maintain the hotel property: carpenters, painters, upholsterers, engineers, electricians, gardeners, and carpet layers.

The maintenance department is also responsible for servicing the heating boilers, air conditioning chilling towers, water softeners, and auxiliary generators. Each major Las Vegas resort has a battery of 250 KW generators, which are used for emergency lighting and elevator operation during power outages.

All these departments are made up of people that the average tourist never sees. Add all the others (dealers, casino supervisors, security, cooks, kitchen helpers, maids, secretaries, public relations, front desk, bellmen, valet attendants, change persons, slot mechanics, waiters, cocktail waitresses, bartenders, hosts, computer operators, PBX operators, human resources) and you can see how easy it is to wind up with 2,600 to 7,000 employees. I know, and there's never one around to tell you where the restrooms are.

What is Nevada's state flower?

The sagebrush. When it dries, it turns into the tumbleweed. Many residents spray paint tumbleweeds in a variety of colors, then use them as decorations outside their covered wagons.

What is the state rock?

The one-point-five carat diamond dinner ring.

What is the state bird?

The mountain bluebird (Sialia Currucoides).

What is the state fish?

The tourist (Pocketus Humongus).

Who was the first celebrity to visit Nevada?

According to historians, it was actress Lola Montez, who came to Truckee Meadows (later Reno) in 1853. In 1984 she changed her name to Joan Collins and starred in the TV show *Dynasty*.

What is the state capital of Nevada?

Carson City, and no it wasn't named for TV star Johnny Carson. Rather, it was in honor of legendary frontier scout Kit Carson—who was Johnny Carson's uncle.

How much water does Las Vegas use?

A whopping 375 gallons per day per person.

Is there a possibility that Las Vegas will run out of water someday?

Under the Boulder Canyon Project Act of 1928, which divided up the Colorado River water among seven western states and Mexico, Nevada is allocated 300,000 acre feet of river water a year. (One acre foot is roughly enough to serve a household of four people for a year.) The last year that records were available, Nevada used about 178,000 square feet of river water. As the population increases, however, water is going to become a major problem.

Different studies are being made—including cloud seeding, sea water desalination, and buying water from other areas. So I don't think Las Vegas will ever run out of water. It will just get more expensive, that's all.

How much of Nevada is owned by the federal government?

Almost 83% of the state is controlled by the feds, or some 60 million acres.

When was gambling legalized in Nevada?

Gambling was legalized on March 19, 1931 by the Nevada Legislature. That same year a bill was signed lowering the residency requirement for a divorce to only six weeks. Now you could lose your money and your honey at the same time!

How many state parks are there in Nevada?

Twenty-two, the largest of which is Valley of Fire, located about an hour northeast of Las Vegas on Interstate 15. Created in 1923, it's also the oldest state park in Nevada.

What percentage of Nevada residents are over 65?

Ten percent of the Silver State's residents have silver in their teeth, silver in their hair, and silver in their pockets.

What is the ratio of men to women in Nevada?

According to the last census, there were 611,880 male residents and 589,953 females in the state.

Who was the first star to appear in a Las Vegas showroom?

I'll give you a hint. Her nickname was "The last of the red-hot mamas." Can't get it? Okay, here's another hint. She sang bawdy songs and told dirty jokes. Still can't get it? All right, here's your last hint. She smoked cigars and had a tattoo of an anchor on her left arm. Yes, it was Sophie Tucker! She premiered at the Last Frontier on the Strip in 1944.

Who was the only U. S. President to appear in a Vegas showroom?

Ronald Reagan, who performed at the Last Frontier in 1954.

What happened to the Last Frontier?

It went bankrupt, after appearances by such performers as Sophie Tucker and Ronald Reagan.

What was the shortest nightclub engagement in Las Vegas history?

Wally Cox (TV's "Mr. Peepers") opened at the Dunes on May 23, 1955, and was paid off after just one show.

What was the first Vegas hotel to present a stage spectacular?

The first hotel to break with the traditional star policy was the Stardust, which presented the Lido de Paris in 1958. The show has been running ever since—hopefully without the same showgirls.

How many cocktail waitresses are there in Las Vegas?

To answer this question, I called the Culinary Union, which represents most of the cocktail waitresses in the city. They didn't even know, but in the union's defense it should be noted that some casinos employ non-union help. A rough estimate would be somewhere between 2,000 and 3,000.

How many dealers are there in Las Vegas?

There are around 4,000 dealers in Las Vegas—and 2,563 of them are named Tony. By the way, here's a breakdown on the number of dealers in top Vegas casinos:

Bally's 360, Treasure Island 430, Monte Carlo 550, Caesars Palace 600, and Bellagio 850. There are three 8-hour shifts in each casino, and dealers usually get a 20-minute break after each hour on the job.

What is the unemployment rate for dealers in Las Vegas?

According to the Nevada State Employment Office, the unemployment rate for dealers is roughly 7 to 10%.

I never seem to see a dealer anywhere in the casino except at the tables. How come?

In most casinos, dealers are not allowed in any public area such as restaurants, public restrooms, lobby, et cetera.   Don't feel sorry for them. They're down in the dealers' break room, talking to their stockbrokers on their cellular telephones.

Is there a big turnover in dealers at Las Vegas casinos?

It's not as bad as it used to be. I remember when a dealer could be fired for talking to a customer, or smiling when a player gave him a tip! Nowadays, employees have some degree of job protection, but a dealer can still get fired.   It's usually for one of the following reasons: stealing, hustling, incompetence, reduction in personnel, arguing with a supervisor, being rude to customers, being late repeatedly, being under the influence of drugs or alcohol, not showing up for work, calling in sick too often (most dealers are allowed 5 sick days a year), and for not following prescribed casino policy. I recently heard of a baccarat dealer losing his $125,000 a year job for stalking an ex-girlfriend, so there are other reasons as well.

How many wedding chapels are there in Las Vegas?

I counted 70 of them in the yellow pages. These include the Drive Up Wedding Window for those who have absolutely nothing to wear, and Weddings on Wheels, which is kind of like ordering a pizza. By the way, there are over 100,000 weddings performed in Las Vegas every year. The busiest day of the week is Saturday, and the most popular day of the year is Valentine's Day, when around 3,000 wedding licenses are issued. (The second most popular wedding date is New Year's Eve.)

No blood test or waiting period is required to get married in Las Vegas. The Marriage License Bureau is open from 8 a.m. until midnight Monday through Thursday, and from 8 a.m. Friday until midnight on Sunday.

How much does it cost to get married in Las Vegas?

Roughly one-half of your income for the rest of your life. But for the wedding itself, the marriage license costs $35 and the civil ceremony at the courthouse runs another $35. Or if you really want to make it a memorable occasion, get married in a balloon. Pilot, crew, minister, six passengers, video tape of ceremony, and flight: $950. (Parachutes, Dramamine, last will and testament are extra.) On average, a Vegas wedding costs around $200.

What kind of sports can I see in Las Vegas?

Professional boxing is probably the biggest attraction for sports fans, with tickets selling for as little as $1,500. Title bouts are usually held at the MGM Grand Garden, Mandalay Bay, or at the Thomas & Mack Center. If one of the fighters is incarcerated at the time, then the bouts are held at the Nevada State Prison.

The UNLV Runnin' Rebels basketball team plays its home games at the Thomas & Mack, consistently winning as many as 8 games a season. Years ago, the Rebels won the NCAA College Championship under the leadership of former coach Jerry Tarkanian, but he was fired for such alleged infractions as recruiting violations, using professional hit men as point guards, and for being an Armenian.

The Las Vegas 51s (named by owner Alfonso "The Enforcer" Giovanni for the number of weeks in a year) play baseball every summer at Cashman Field. A member of the Pacific Coast League, this triple-A team has set many records over the years: crowd attendance, team batting average, most pitchers used in a single game, and highest price ever charged for a chili dog.

Want to see a little calf roped and dragged to the ground by a big cowboy on a horse? Why then, it's the National Finals Rodeo each December at the Thomas & Mack. It lasts for ten days, but you've got to get tickets at least a year in advance. Believe it or not, it's more popular than the Super Bowl, but if you ask me it's a lot of bull.

Racing fans now have the Las Vegas Motor Speedway, which has a seating capacity for 107,000. Finished in 1996, the speedway is already drawing such racing stars as Terry and Bobby Labonte, whom I got a chance to meet recently when they were in town for the Las Vegas 300. Here's a tape recording of our interview:

Terry, how fast does your car go?
I'm Bobby. He's Terry.
Oh, sorry. Bobby, how fast does your car go?
Pretty fast.
Faster than a hundred miles an hour?
Yeah.
Two hundred miles an hour?
Yeah.
So what do you think about when you're going that fast?
Nothin' I'm just concentratin' on my drivin' and readin' my gauges.

And what if you need to change tires or something?

Well, I can communicate with my crew, see, and then I just tell 'em I'm comin' in, and then I come in.

Uh huh, and how long does it take to change a tire?

Uh, about ten seconds.

So to change all four, it would take . . . 40 seconds?

Yeah, I guess so.

And what do you think about when they're changing your tires?

AW, FOR CRYIN' OUT LOUD, I AIN'T THINKIN' ABOUT.............

Unfortunately, the tape ran out at this point, but this gives you an idea of how exciting the sport of auto racing can be.

How many golf courses are there in Las Vegas?

There are 30 golf courses in the Las Vegas area, which takes in Green Valley, Henderson, and Boulder City. You can reserve your own tee time on any course or use a booking service (in the yellow pages under Golf Tournament and Booking Service). For best times, call a day ahead.

Golf can be a dangerous sport, with golf balls reaching speeds of up to 75 miles an hour. That's why I always wear a helmet when I play. Unnecessary noise, such as people hollering "Fore!", can throw off your putting game. That's why I always wear ear muffs when I play. Insects and snakes can also be a problem. That's why I always wear body armor and hip boots when I play. Remember, too, that golf is a leisure activity, so be prepared to see people wearing outlandish outfits.

Which golf course is the most expensive?

The most expensive golf course is the $45 million Shadow Creek course, which costs $1,000 a person—but the price includes 18 holes of golf with cart and caddy, limousine to and from the course, and a one-bedroom suite overnight at the Mirage. If that's too much for you, then buy a golf shirt with the Shadow Creek insignia on it. That's only $165.

How busy is McCarran International Airport?

McCarran gets an average of 840 commercial flights every day of the year! Based on passenger activity (28 million a year), that makes it one of the ten busiest airports in the country. There are also 5,000 cars a day vying for the 400 parking spaces, so do like I do. Take a rental car to the airport, park in a red zone, and then report it stolen.

What are some of the stupidest things I can do in Las Vegas?

After 30 years in the trenches, and seeing just about everything, here's my list:

- Gambling when you're drinking
- Gambling when you're tired
- Gambling when you're mad
- Gambling when you're sleepy
- Gambling to get back your losses
- Gambling when you're hungry
- Gambling to kill time
- Gambling

Index